Competency to Stand Trial and Mental Illness

Competency to Stand Trial and Mental Illness

Laboratory of Community Psychiatry
Harvard Medical School

Foreword by
SALEEM A. SHAH

Jason Aronson   **New York**

345.7304
H339c
1974

This monograph was written by a recognized authority in the subject matter field under project number 7R01-MH-18112-01 from the National Institute of Mental Health. The opinions expressed herein are the views of the author and do not necessarily reflect the official position of the National Institute of Mental Health or the Department of Health, Education, and Welfare.

ISBN: 87668-190-9

L.C.: 74-25406

©1974 Jason Aronson, Inc.

DHEW Publication No. (ADM) 74–103
(Formerly DHEW Publication No. (HSM) 73–9105)
Printed 1973   Reprinted 1974

Foreword

Among the various issues around which the legal and mental health systems frequently interact, perhaps no subject has received, more attention than the defense of insanity. The trial of the insanity defense, it has been noted, seems to be treated as if it were "a contemporary morality play revolving around the issues of sickness and guilt" (Goldstein 1967). However, Morris and Hawkins were moved to comment that "Rivers of ink, mountains of printers' lead, and forests of paper have been expended on an issue that is surely marginal to the chaotic problems of the effective, rational, and humane prevention and treatment of crime" (Morris and Hawkins 1970). While these authors have obviously felt compelled to resort to hyperbole to make their point, the comment is consistent with the fact that the insanity defense is raised in fewer than two percent of all cases coming for jury trial (Morris and Hawkins 1970), and less than one percent of all felony dispositions (Matthews 1970).

In marked contrast to the relative rarity of the defense of insanity, the issue of competency to stand trial is far more frequently raised and affects literally thousands of persons who are committed each year to mental hospitals for study and/or treatment. For example, at least 5800 persons were so affected in 1967 (Scheidemandel and Kanna 1969). The survey which provided the above information also revealed that of all persons committed to state mental institutions in 1967, fully 52 percent were there for study and/or treatment in regard to the issue of pretrial competency. Only four percent were there because they had been found not guilty by reason of insanity (Scheidemandel and Kanno 1969). Fairly similar findings were obtained in a subsequent survey conducted a couple of years later (Eckerman 1972).

The question about an accused person's competency to stand trial typically arises rather early in the criminal process, the issue is rather easily (even too easily) raised by various participants in the process, and, when such determinations result in a judicial finding of incompetency, the resulting indeterminate confinement in a mental hospital may in many instances terminate the criminal proceedings for all practical purposes.

v

Previous studies suggest that the basic common law criteria pertaining to the question of pretrial competency are in many instances poorly understood by psychiatrists as well as by lawyers. The issue of competency to stand trial is often confused with that of criminal responsibility — the defendant's mental condition at the time of the alleged act. Moreover, the injection of various psychiatric considerations as well as the use of an assortment of legal strategies by attorneys, tends to further confuse and confound the basic question about the defendant's competency. In view of the fact that a judicial finding of incompetency typically results in involuntary and indeterminate confinement to a mental hospital, there are many questions which need to be addressed in regard to gaining better understanding of the basic issues involved, the development of reliable and easy to use assessment procedures, the use of less costly and less confining diagnostic and treatment facilities, as well as fundamental considerations of fairness and the protection of Constitutional rights.

The specific objectives of the research described in this report were the development, validation, and demonstration of quantifiable clinical criteria for the assessment of competency to stand trial. Following the development and testing of the assessment instruments, the project moved on to provide training and also to facilitate implementation of the products of the research to personnel in the mental health and criminal justice systems of Massachusetts.

The impact of the study for mental health and legal policies and practices goes considerably beyond simply the development of the aforementioned assessment instruments. The research indicates that findings of pretrial competency have, in the past, been made far too frequently. "Valid incompetency for trial," the investigators point out, "is a rather rare phenomenon." For example, in 1971 Bridgewater State Hospital found only six persons out of 501 observational cases referred, to be incompetent. However, in 1963 the Hospital had found about 22 percent of such cases to be incompetent.

There are a number of rather important recommendations provided in the following report in regard to various service programs as well as concerning related policies. The findings emanating from this research have already contributed to some major reformulations of legal and mental health policies. The principal investigator (Dr. A. Louis McGarry) and the co-principal investigator (Prof. William J. Curran) were closely involved in drafting sections of The Mental Health Reform Act of 1970 which went into effect in Massachusetts as of November 1, 1971. As a result of this Act and related developments in case law, the investigators estimate that there were about 1,000 fewer admissions in 1972 to Massachusetts mental hospitals for pretrial competency examinations. Similarly, and partly over the life of the research project, the percentage of persons found incompetent to stand trial in the State dropped from about 22 percent of the cases examined (in 1963) to about six percent in 1970.

In conclusion, this is a rather significant piece of empirical research in an important area of law and mental health interaction. Our objective in publishing this report is to facilitate the wide dissemination of the findings and to enable legal and mental health professionals, program administrators, and policy-makers, to utilize the products of this work for seeking necessary improvements in various programs and policies in regard to the issue of pretrial competency.

Saleem A. Shah
Chief, Center for Studies
of Crime and Delinquency

REFERENCES

Eckerman, W.C. *A Nationwide Survey of Mental Health and Correctional Institutions for Adult Mentally Disordered Offenders.* DHEW Publication No. (HSM) 73-9018. Washington, D.C.: U.S. Government Printing Office, 1972.

Goldstein, A.S. *The Insanity Defense.* New Haven: Yale University Press, 1967.

Matthews, A.R. *Mental Disability and the Criminal Law.* Chicago: American Bar Foundation, 1970.

Morris, N. and Hawkins, G. *The Honest Politician's Guide to Crime Control.* Chicago: University of Chicago Press, 1970.

Scheidemandel, P.L., and Kanno, C.K. *The Mentally Ill Offender: A Survey of Treatment Programs.* Washington, D.C.: The Joint Information Service, American Psychiatric Association, 1969.

Laboratory of Community Psychiatry
Harvard Medical School

PROJECT STAFF

* A. Louis McGarry, M. D., Principal Investigator
* William J. Curran, S.M.Hyg., J.D., Co-principal Investigator
* Paul D. Lipsitt, LL.B., Ph.D., Research Director
* David Lelos, M.A., Research Psychologist
* Ralph Schwitzgebel, Ed.D., J.D., Research Psychologist
* Arthur H. Rosenberg, LL.M., J.D., Research Attorney
  Eugene Balcanoff, M.D., Research Psychiatrist
  Fred Bender, LL.B., Research Attorney
  Richard Bendt, M.D., Research Psychiatrist
  Neil Chayet, LL.B., Research Attorney

RESEARCH ASSISTANTS

Sarah Clark, B.A.
Leslie Clemons, M.S.
Douglas Goldman, B.S.
Deborah Lowrance
Nancy Lundy, B.A.
Marie Noerdlinger, B.A.
Dori Slater, B.A.
Nancy Talbott
Susan Wojcik, B.A.
Cynthia Rego, A.B.

SECRETARIES

* Marie del Rosario
  Joyce Bailes
  Nancy Jacobs

---

*Active on the project at the time of the final report.

Contents

CHAPTER I

Summary and Conclusions of the Project

A. The Problem

Historically, competency to stand trial is based on our English common law heritage, holding that a person must have the capacity to adequately defend himself against his accusers in a court of law. The criteria for this capacity include an understanding of the nature of the legal process, a recognition of the consequences that could follow from the accusation, and the ability to assist legal counsel in one's own defense. These criteria are intended to provide due process of law safeguards.

Most frequently the alleged incompetency of criminal defendants is raised on the basis of possible mental illness. It is evident from our own preliminary work and that of others (McGarry 1965; Hess and Thomas 1963; Settle and Oppergard 1964) that great confusion has reigned and irrelevant medical criteria have been applied to the determination of competency by the psychiatric profession on whom the burden has fallen to provide expert examination and testimony on the issue. It has become equally apparent that the courts themselves have often confused the criteria for competency with the separate and different legal criteria for criminal responsibility. This confusion about the criteria for competency by psychiatry and the law has been compounded by a lack of relevant communication on the issue between the disciplines of psychiatry and law.

There is certainly nothing new in the observation that the disciplines of psychiatry and the law have had difficulty in communicating with each other. To suggest that the central problem is one of communication, two ways, is to observe the obvious. It is none the less so. Thus, when a court takes the trouble (which it usually doesn't) to articulate the tripartite common law criteria for competency and gets back the answer "Schizophrenia," we are witnessing the interdisciplinary lack of rational communication which has governed the handling of the competency issue in this country with rare exceptions.

1

The result has been that many people, who have been judged to be incompetent for trial, have been unnecessarily and inaccurately committed to our mental hospitals and denied their right to trial. These commitments have proven to be stigmatizing and anti-therapeutic. It is clear, in Massachusetts at least, that these committed incompetents, without trial, have been subjected to society's severest sanctions against both the criminal and the mentally ill and in the past have been provided with the safeguards of neither.

Recent publications have given us a clearer picture of the dimensions of the competency issue nationwide. In the first place, in terms of people whose lives and freedom are affected, competency is a vastly more important issue than criminal responsibility.[1]

Matthews (1966) reported that the use of these procedures has been growing. Given the very crowded and growing calendars of our courts and the general lack of satisfaction with our penal system it is not surprising that there should be increased pressure for seeking alternatives. Generally competency procedures are easily invoked (and constitutionally required when there is any doubt),[2] time-saving as far as the court is concerned. As this project and the work of others has documented, however, this well-meant set of motivations has led to excessive use of these procedures with destructive consequences for the patient-defendants involved and at great and wasteful expense to the public treasury.

In recent years there has been growing pressure from civil liberty advocates to do away with involuntary civil commitment of the mentally ill, or at least to tighten and narrow the standards for involuntary commitment or make the procedures more complex and onerous. The recently passed Lanterman-Petris-Short Act in California is an example of the latter. One practical consequence of these changes is the sharply increased alternative use of the criminal process and pretrial mental hospital commitment for the mentally ill. It is a simple matter to allege "disturbing the peace" and order an admission of a mentally ill person as an alternative to complex and restrictive civil procedures. Thus at Metropolitan State Hospital

---

1. Thus in Massachusetts in fiscal year 1970 there were 2,101 mental hospitalizations pretrial and no commitments posttrial as not guilty by reason of insanity. Nationwide it is estimated that of 29,000 mental hospitalizations in 1967, 15,000 were for incompetency and 1,450 were as a result of not guilty by reason of insanity verdicts (Scheidemandel and Kanno 1969). It is our impression that the latter statistic is highly inflated, (see table IV in the reference). But there is wide variation from one jurisdiction to the next. Whereas Massachusetts had 2,101 observational admissions in F.Y. 1970 (14.2 percent of all admissions to Massachusetts mental hospitals) MacDonald (1969) reports that in 17 years of his extensive forensic experience in Colorado the issue of competency for trial has been raised only once.

2. Pate v. Robinson, 383 U.S. 375 (1966).

2

serving Los Angeles, pretrial competency commitments have increased six-fold since the new act.[3] The effect is to criminalize the treatment of the mentally ill. Other jurisdictions which may be embarking on a similar escalation of the use of pretrial competency procedures will do well to read this record of Massachusett's mistakes, abuses and agonizing reforms in this area.

B. Specific Objectives of the Project

The specific objectives of the project were to develop, validate, and demonstrate quantifiable clinical criteria for competency to stand trial. What was needed were instruments designed to accurately assess competency, conceptualized and expressed in language with sufficient familiarity to both the law and psychiatry to provide a basis for relevant communication and assessment of the issue.

In this project, a multidisciplinary team consisting of lawyers, psychiatrists, and psychologists tested, interviewed, and observed persons referred to the Bridgewater State Hospital for a pretrial examination for competency. The team tapped into the legal system at several points, including the initial observation admission, the competency hearing, and the trial in those cases where the defendant had been returned for trial rather than indefinitely committed as incompetent for trial.

Independent of the assessment and evaluations made by the service personnel (judges and psychiatrists) in the system, the research team constructed, adminstered, and evaluated several instruments designed to determine more concretely and quantifiably a person's capacity and ability to cope with the task of performing as a defendant in a criminal trial.[4] These assessments were then compared with the ongoing decisions made by the criminal justice system in an attempt to establish their accuracy and validity.

Subsequent to the research, instrument development, and testing phases of this project (September 1, 1966 to December 31, 1970), the project moved on to training and implementing the products of the research in the mental health and criminal justice systems of Massachusetts (January 1, 1970 to December 31, 1972).

---

3. Personal communication, Seymour Pollack, M.D., University of Southern California.

4. See Chapter III, "Methodology," and Chapter IV, "Comprehensive Results, Validation, and Products of the Project."

C. Significant Conclusions and Products of the Project

The research and documentation which support the conclusions arrived at are contained in the text which follows this subsection of the report. The salient conclusions arrived at in this project are as follows:

1. Brief screening examinations on the issue of competency can prevent many unnecessary admissions to mental hospitals, particularly if such instruments as the Competency Screening Test (CST) and the Competency Assessment Instrument (CAI), developed by the project (see below) are utilized.

2. The legal criteria for competency to stand trial can be accurately translated into psychological and clinical terms and retranslated into relevant legally oriented data.

3. Psychiatrists who are knowledgeable about the criminal justice system and the relevant criteria for competency to stand trial, can effectively serve the courts on the issue.

4. Incompetency to stand trial on the basis of mental illness is rare and is usually quickly responsive to treatment.

5. In Massachusetts, excessive conservatism regarding release and excessive restrictiveness in management have governed the care and treatment of alleged offenders committed as incompetent to stand trial.

6. The mental health system in Massachusetts, although there have been recent improvements, has consistently required higher standards of competency than relevant case law would indicate is required. There appears to be a bias among mental health professionals against returning defendants for trial.

7. Civil commitment of mentally ill alleged offenders led to significantly shorter mental hospitalizations than for comparable incompetent defendants who were committed under criminal sanctions with charges still outstanding. In the latter group, hospitalization tended to be excessively prolonged.

8. Unless criminal charges can be otherwise disposed of, it is in the best interest of the mentally ill defendants to stand trial as expeditiously as possible.

9. The interpersonal skills and sustained involvement of defense counsel are important and overlooked factors in the functioning competency of mentally ill defendants. A skillful, supportive attorney who devotes adequate time to working with mentally ill defendants can maximally facilitate the coping strengths of such defendants. The converse is equally true.

4

10. A Competency Screening Test (CST) has been developed which provides a summative score of competency to stand trial (see Appendix A). Interrater reliability of the scoring of this instrument has been established (interrater R of .93). The major usefulness of the instrument is seen as screening out the clearly competent so that more extensive and intensive examination and work-up of the competency of defendants would be unnecessary. At its present stage of development a score above 20 on this instrument should create a very strong presumption of competency. Further examination, and particularly mental hospitalization in such a case, is justified only on unusual grounds which should be adequately articulated. This instrument has now been translated into vernacular Spanish and modified into a feminine version.

11. A legal psychiatric instrument, the Competency Assessment Instrument (CAI), has been developed (see Appendix B) which provides quantifiable criteria for competency to stand trial. The instrument is an attempt at an assessment of all possible legal grounds for a finding of incompetency. It is expressed as a series of thirteen ego functions related to what is required of a defendant in criminal proceedings in order that he may adequately cope with and protect himself in such proceedings. Interrater reliability has been established with this instrument. (The overall reliability coefficient of the latest version is .87.) This instrument has been demonstrated in the courtroom to be a feasible and effective basis for interdisciplinary communication about and assessment of competency to stand trial.

Based on an evaluation of the training of 216 clinicians in the use of the CAI during the training phase of this project, it appears that the use of the CAI, with interviews structured around its thirteen items (a *Handbook* with definitions and a structured interview protocol has been produced — see Appendix B), can produce satisfactorily high interrater reliability (R of .84) *without* extensive training (see Chapter IV, F. "Training Activities and Their Evaluation"). Very high levels of interrater reliability can be attained in the use of the CAI with its *Handbook* if an extended series of patient-defendants are examined and rated using feedback and consensus-seeking techniques.

12. Serious abuses of due process in the use of competency procedures in the Massachusetts criminal justice system have been found by the project and largely corrected.

13. When civil measures for the mental hospital commitment of the mentally ill are procedurally onerous and criminal proceddures less so, there is a likelihood that the criminal route for the commitment of the mentally ill will be used excessively. In Massachusetts the decision to hospitalize for a competency workup originates, in large measure, from the judge, and the grounds for such admissions appear to be inadequately reviewed by the judge or challenged by defense counsel.

14. Inappropriate and unnecessary mental hospitalizations on the competency issue appear to rise largely from over-taxed courts seeking alternatives to the penal system.

15. The great majority of defense counsel interviewed in this project were not aware of the common law criteria for competency to stand trial.

16. The common law criteria for competency for trial appear to apply in the statutory and case law of all American legal jurisdictions with minor variations. However, there continues to be confusion in many jurisdictions between the criteria for competency and those for criminal responsibility. Competency criteria are elementary, vague, and of little help to the examining psychiatrist. Attempts by appellate courts to define criteria more precisely, particularly the *degree* of capacity or incapacity which establishes competency or incompetency, have been inconsistent and idiosyncratic.

17. There is great variation and much vagueness among American legal jurisdictions both in terms of the weight of evidence required to make a finding of incompetency, and once the incompetency issue is raised, whether the presumption is one of competency or incompetency. Insofar as it can be discerned, most jurisdictions appear to make the rebuttable presumption that once the issue is raised the defendant is incompetent and his competency must be proved (usually by the prosecution). This is likely to weight in the direction of a finding of incompetency.

18. Although there is an abundance of case law and statutes citing mental illness as a basis for a finding of incompetency for trial, there is a paucity which cite mental retardation. It is our impression that the competency issue is raised too often for the mentally ill and too infrequently for the mentally retarded.

19. Massachusetts' new Mental Health Reform Act of 1970 (effective date November 1, 1971), which had significant input from this project (the principal investigator and co-principal investigator were the primary draftsmen of the

6

Act), has had a striking impact, particularly on competency procedures. (See Chapter VI, B. "The Mental Health Reform Act of 1970") Based on the statistics of the first 6 months under the new Act and projected for its first year, there will be 1,000 fewer admissions annually to Massachusetts mental hospitals for competency workups. In addition, the number of prolonged commitments arising from these observational admissions will have been halved (from 76 in fiscal year 1971 to about 40 for the first year under the new Act).

This section of the report has been limited to the *salient* conclusions and products of the project. A more detailed account of our conclusions may be obtained by reading the published papers supported by the project. Readers who are interested in recommended procedural and substantive *reforms* in the area of competency should read Chapter VII, subsection D. "Necessary and Recommended Reforms."

CHAPTER II

Research Design of the Project

A. An Interdisciplinary Approach

It was concluded that since the competency issue involved at least three disciplines, psychiatry, psychology, and law, an interdisciplinary approach was obviously called for. The principal investigator and the co-principal investigator were a psychiatrist and a lawyer respectively. The discipline of psychology rounded out the team both for clinical purposes and research methodology. Initially, the discipline of social work was included in the expectation that field work and family study would complete the study of a given defendant-patient and his lifestyle. As the work progressed, however, its focus increasingly narrowed to the issue of competency *per se*, and the contributions of the social worker, although useful, did not appear to be essential and were dispensed with. Social work contributions are seen as essential to dispositional planning and would have reappeared in the fourth year of our original 5-year plan when broader clinical responsibilities would have been shouldered in the demonstration phase of the project. But this was not to be since the initial grant support was cut back to 4 years.

B. Legal and Ethical Context of the Research

Permission to conduct the research at the Bridgewater State Hospital and the courts of the Commonwealth was obtained from the Chief Justice of the Superior Court, the Superintendant of Bridgewater, and the Commissioner of Correction. But research in the criminal justice system carries unusual risks, particularly regarding the preservation of the confidentiality of potentially incriminating material. Most jurisdictions do not provide for privilege regarding research and data are therefore subject to subpoena. Massachusetts has an interesting statute (*General Laws*, Chapter 111, Section 24A) which gives to the Commissioner of Public Health the authority to declare "scientific studies and research which have for their purpose the reduction of morbidity and mortality within the Commonwealth" to be privileged.

An alternative to an attempt to invoke this authority (the Commissioner of Public Health), which is a relatively unique provision,[1] is to seek the sanction of criminal justice authorities in advance of the research and obtain an agreement that under given conditions the confidentiality of the research will be respected by prosecutorial authorities. Of course, this might not protect us from defense subpoena, but in line with Morris's principle of less severity (Morris 1966; Schwitzgebel 1968), such an invasion of the data would be seen as likely to ameliorate rather than exacerbate consequences to the defendant if defense counsel called on and used such data.

We chose a strategy which comprises another alternative, and that is, that the data did not represent reliable and valid evidence regarding competency *during* the research and was therefore not "within reasonable medical certainty" and not credible. Secondly, the position was taken that the data related only to competency and was not relevant to criminal responsibility.

We then proceeded to present our design to the Review Committee at the Law-Medicine Institute[2] as required by the Surgeon General's regulations. One of the members of the Committee challenged us at this point to the effect that we could hardly claim "informed consent" from defendants whose competency was the very issue we were inquiring into. We responded to this challenge with a letter to the National Institute of Mental Health further justifying the contention that confidentiality would be protected and that an exception to the "informed consent" requirement was in order. Thè argument turned on basically four facts:

1. It was vital for the research that we have access precisely to defendants who might not be capable of "informed consent."

2. Project personnel were acting under the authority and with the sanction of the court.

3. Quotations from the *Congressional Record* indicated that it was the intent of Congress to make an exception in the "informed consent" requirement for pretrial examination of

---

1. See also the *Maryland Annotated Code*, Article 43, Section 149-C; Article 35, Section 102; and Article 75-C, Section 11; and *Connecticut Public Acts* (1969), Public Act Number 819, Sections 5 and 6.

2. The original grantee for this project was the Law-Medicine Institute of Boston University. The project subsequently was transferred to the Laboratory of Community Psychiatry, Harvard Medical School, where it was completed.

Federal prisoners and that this was analogous to our situation in Massachusetts.

4. Our defendant-subjects were protected from self-incrimination by Massachusetts General Laws 233, Section 23B.

The National Institute of Mental Health ultimately agreed to the request for an exception by letter and we were able to go forward. In the approving letter from NIMH it was stressed that, in their view, the project was operating under the legitimizing authority of the court.

Consistent with our agreement with the Chief Justice of the Superior Court, all of these patient-defendants were advised that their participation would not affect their case one way or another. With very few exceptions, the men did agree to participate. In each case an attempt was made to contact the defense counsel to get his clearance. On no occasion did defense counsel object; indeed most participated themselves in the competency posttrial attorney protocol. In many cases, however, defense counsel was not active in the case during the first week at Bridgewater. Only two attempts were made by defense counsel to involve project staff in actual criminal proceedings. This was resisted on the basis that the work was experimental and had not been validated and could not be presented as credible evidence. The attorneys did not persist. We have been completely successful in carrying out our pledge to our examinees that our data would be both confidential and privileged. On a number of occasions project staff were approached by the professional staff at Bridgewater and requested to divulge our data and findings to them in order to assist them in their deliberations. This would have violated the research design which called for the research data to be completely independent and blind from the Bridgewater staff's workup, and we successfully resisted on those grounds.

C. The 5-Year Plan and a Chronology of Events and Studies Undertaken During the Initial 4 Years of Research Support

Initially, a 5-year project was planned: *year one* was designed to permit the psychiatrists on the grant to thoroughly familiarize themselves with the realities of the courtroom and the legal process. Many trials were attended and defendants and their attorneys interviewed and followed through the actual criminal process. The activities during the year were focused in the Suffolk Superior Criminal Court of Boston. Since the Massachusetts Superior Court is a circuit riding system (except for the Chief Justice who remains at Suffolk), we were able to observe a variety of judges and cases

10

during the year and experience the realities of the criminal justice process. One paper was published out of this experience (Balcanoff 1969).

Also during the first year, we were occupied with the development of new instruments in order to articulate the criteria for competency. These instruments will be described in detail below (Chapter III, "Methodology"). Our purpose in their design was to develop, from relevant clinical and psychological data, the functions (ego functions if you will) which relate to what is realistically required of a defendant to adequately protect himself in the trial process. We also wanted to translate these data into language and concepts which would provide a relevant and common basis for communication between clinicians and the judiciary.

The first of the two followup studies of the project began during the first year. We chose to follow up the fate of the patient-defendants at Boston State Hospital in 1960 whom the principal investigator had studied. A paper which was subsequently published arose from this work (McGarry 1969).

During the second year we began our work at Bridgewater with a representative sample of patient-defendants hospitalized on the issue of competency to stand trial. By this time, prototypes of a series of new clinical and psychological instruments had been developed. These included (1) the Competency Assessment Instrument (CAI), comprised of thirteen quantifiable items relating to functions expected of an adequately coping defendant; (2) a sentence completion test (CST) with stems derived from a defendant's role in criminal proceedings and modeled after the Stotsky-Weinberg instrument (Dr. Weinberg consulted with us in its development); (3) a projective instrument modeled after the TAT in which pictures of courtroom scenes are used; (4) a social responsibility test designed to capture patient-defendants' attitudes toward authority and limits; and (5) a make-believe case designed to elicit a narrative relative to the defendant's understanding of the criminal justice system. In addition, we experimented with at least two standardized clinical ego function tests, but these were soon discarded for reasons of economy of time and lack of relevance to competency *per se*. The standard mental status form developed at Boston State Hospital was substituted. In addition to the new instruments which were defined and modified during the year, a standard battery of psychological tests was administered to the patient-defendants who were examined.

During this year the psychology staff sought out several control populations in order to establish base-line date and compare the results on the sentence completion instrument (CST) with later

Bridgewater samples. A distribution of scores on the CST was then established.

Added to what has been noted above were a courtroom observation protocol (designed to organize observations of an actual trial or hearing), a posttrial interview protocol for the patient-defendant (designed to capture the defendant's reality testing and attitudes regarding the actual court experience), and a posttrial defense attorney protocol (designed to capture the defense attorney's sophistication regarding competency and his evaluation of the defendant's actual performance).

In the design of the study, the pretrial psychological testing was separate and blind from the pretrial psychiatric workup. The courtroom observation and posttrial defendant and defense attorney protocols were also separate and blind from the pretrial workups. The posttrial workups were adminsitered by a research attorney.

The Competency Assessment Instrument (CAI) was generally completed by two or more psychiatrists on the same patient at the same time during pretrial, but the scoring of the instrument was done independently by the several observers. During the posttrial workup, the research attorney (on occasion accompanied by a psychiatrist from the research staff who was seeing the defendant for the first time) also scored the CAI instrument independently, without seeing the pretrial scorings.

During the second year, 51 patient-defendants were seen at Bridgewater. This population was regarded as generally representative of all the men sent there for competency workups. We found that only where men were actually psychotic or at least moderately retarded, did a serious question of competency arise. There were only a handful of such men among those we examined during that year.

By the end of the year we had established the basic sequence and variety of data which it was decided was necessary and valuable in researching the competency issue. An outline of the data we elected to collect follows:

Pretrial Schedule of Protocols

A. Research Psychiatrists
   1. Identifying (demographic) face sheet data
   2. Formal mental status — diagnosis
   3. Competency Assessment Instrument (CAI)[3]

B. Research Psychologist
   1. Competency Screening Test (CST)[3]

---

3. This material was not shared among the staff except at extended intervals.

2. Courtroom Apperception Test (CRAT)[4]
3. Rorschach
4. Graham Kendall
5. MMPI
6. Wechsler
7. Draw-a-Person
8. Social Responsibility Test
9. Make-believe Case
C. Research Attorney
1. Competency Assessment Instrument (CAI)[4]

Trial Schedule of Protocols
A. Research Psychiatrist
1. Courtroom observation protocol
B. Research Attorney
1. Courtroom observation protocol

Posttrial Schedule of Protocols
A. Research Psychiatrist
1. Competency Assessment Instrument (CAI)[4]
B. Research Attorney
1. Posttrial defendant protocol
2. Posttrial attorney protocol
3. Competency Assessment Instrument (CAI)[4]
(after 1 and 2)

An ancillary study was begun by the legal staff of the grant. It consisted of a legal review, updating case law and statutory law on the competency issue in the fifty states and Federal jurisdictions.

During the third year, we chose to focus on a sample of seriously disabled men. We concluded from the experience of the previous year that there was a serious question of competency only where severe mental disability existed, such as active psychosis or moderate to severe mental retardation.

In reviewing our experience at Bridgewater, it appeared that approximately 50 men a year, of this degree of pathology, were sent to Bridgewater for competency workups. We, therefore, elected to focus the work on the anticipated 50 men who manifested severe pathology and were most likely to pose a serious question of competency. Each week the team reviewed the admission descriptions of new pretrial observational admissions. Approximately 450 men were screened in this fashion. Fifty-three men were screened into the study population and about 400 out of it. In many cases, the screening of the records was followed by a

---

4. This material was not shared among the staff except at extended intervals.

screening examination after which men were either excluded as being obviously competent or included as manifesting severe pathology. The study population was then given the complete workup which is outlined above. Massachusetts law at that time (General Laws Chapter 123, Sections 100 and 105) provided for a 35-day admission for pretrial observation. The pretrial workup of the project generally took place during the first 2 weeks of this period.

Early in the third year we were informed by NIMH that our grant would be supported for 4 rather than 5 years. The design had called for the fourth year to be a demonstration year in which the project staff and the Bridgewater staff would assume full clinical responsibility in doing competency workups and bringing what had been learned into the courtroom. Such an opportunity arose in the spring of 1969. Legal actions had been brought challenging the legality of the indefinite commitments of 15 men who were committed to Bridgewater while awaiting trial. These actions were based on the Rohrer decision of the Massachusetts Supreme Judicial Court[5] which set down the requirements of notice and a hearing before such indefinite commitments could constitutionally take place. The project staff participated in these hearings and the Competency Assessment Instrument (CAI) was the basis for expert testimony on the competency issue. The Competency Screening Test was also utilized. (This activity is described in greater detail in Chapter IV, "Comprehensive Results, Validation, and Products of the Project.")

In addition, by special appointment of Chief Justice Tauro of the Superior Court, the grant team was authorized as *amicus curiae* to examine one, Dennis Ford, on the question of his competency to stand trial. We were pleased to accept this charge since Mr. Ford was mentally retarded and our legal research had revealed that very little appellate attention had been paid to the competency of the retarded to stand criminal trial. It was anticipated that the Ford case would be appealed to the Supreme Judicial Court. There are good grounds to speculate that retardates are a good deal less able to cope adequately with criminal trial than the mentally ill. This speculation is based both on the cognitive deficits of the retarded and their characteristic dependency and malleability which permits them to be easily manipulated by investigatory and prosecutory personnel. An extensive evaluation was prepared which discussed the Competency Screening Test and the Competency Assessment Instrument (CAI) as they applied to Ford's competency. Chief Justice Tauro accepted into evidence the evaluation and the

---

5. Petition of Rohrer, 353 Mass. 282, 230 N.E. 2nd 915 (1967).

testimony of Dr. Eugene Balcanoff of the competency team. Ford's attorney at this point decided that it was not in his client's best interest to appeal the finding of incompetency.

Also during the third year, a demographic study was begun of the entire population sent to Bridgewater during years two and three. This study was undertaken partly for actuarial purposes — to determine the rates of competency-incompetency in the Bridgewater population that could be reliably compared to rates in comparable populations in other jurisdictions. Another purpose was to discover demographic variables which might be significantly related to competency and incompetency.

During the fourth year the analysis of the data and preparation for publication was the focus of our work.[6] Two papers were presented at the May, 1970, meeting of the American Psychiatric Association and subsequently published (McGarry 1971; Lipsitt, Lelos, and McGarry 1971) in the *American Journal of Psychiatry*. One paper was a followup of the men returned for trial from Bridgewater in 1964–1966, and the other was a description of the Competency Screening Test and the results of its use with the third year Bridgewater sample as compared with several control groups. A third paper presented at the annual meeting of the American Psychiatric Association in Washington, D.C., in May, 1971, and later published in the *American Journal of Psychiatry* (Rosenberg and McGarry 1972) dealt with qualifications for expert witness status on the competency issue.

In our fourth year work, a particular attempt was made to establish the reliability of the several test instruments, develop handbooks for their use, and establish the validity of these instruments. This work will be described more completely below (Chapters III and IV). The CAI in particular was tightened and redesigned, and more concentrated attention was given to its *handbook*. In addition, factor analyses, regression analyses, and discriminate analyses of the data were conducted (see Chapter IV).

In the summer of 1970, we received an extension of grant support by administrative supplement for 4 months. The termination date moved to December 31, 1970. We took this opportunity to continue to analyze the data and to prepare the final report. This time was used to go back to Bridgewater for two main objectives. One was a successful attempt to establish cross-observer and cross-discipline reliability of the redesigned CAI instrument and the completion of the *handbook* for that instrument (see Chapters III

---

6. During year four the project Grantee was changed from the Boston University Law-Medicine Institute to the Laboratory of Community Psychiatry, Harvard Medical School.

and IV and Appendix B). The second major objective was the development of a new, reliable, and valid multiple-choice, forced-choice instrument. The CST was transposed into a multiple-choice test, selecting items that had been given various scores, so that each multiple-choice item included 2's, 1's, and 0's. This method would have simplified the administration and scoring if it had been successful.

The forced-choice method was not effective, since it did not discriminate competent from incompetent individuals. Shifting from the semiprojective nature of the open-ended sentence-completion test to multiple-choice produced a leveling of scores in the 22-item test that did not differentiate competent and incompetent defendants. Therefore, this line of test construction was not pursued.

D. Implementation and Training Phase of the Project

Following the research and instrument development phase of the project described above, further support was provided (from January 1971 through December 31, 1972) in order to train mental health professionals in the use of the new instruments (CST and CAI), and to introduce their use in the mental health and criminal justice systems in Massachusetts.

Specific objectives of the implementation and training phase were as follows:

1. To refine the Competency Assessment Instrument (CAI) and its manual;
2. To establish adequate interrater reliability in the use of the CAI;
3. To train mental health professionals in the use of the CST and CAI;
4. To introduce the use of our instruments in the mental health and criminal justice systems in Massachusetts;
5. To prepare and disseminate a brief (25 to 30 pages) account of our work for purposes of introductory training;
6. To complete and disseminate a comprehensive final report with an evaluation of the effectiveness of our training efforts; and
7. To prepare video training tapes for the use of the Competency Assessment Instrument (CAI).

We chose as the particular targets of our training the two mental health institutions which had been the principal sites of our research (Bridgewater State Hospital and Boston State Hospital) and the four other State Hospitals which appeared to have rates of incompetency up to 1970 which were too high (Northampton, Metropolitan, Gardner and Taunton State Hospitals). The hospitals provided good geographic coverage of Massachusetts.

One-and-one-half-day training institutes were planned covering each of these institutions. Mental health professionals throughout the State were given notice of the times and places of the training and were invited to attend.

The ultimate design of the training activities was as follows:

1. In advance of the training (one to two weeks) one-half of the clinicians expected to attend were randomly selected and mailed copies of the CAI instrument and its *Handbook* (Appendix B), and were instructed to study the *Handbook* in preparation for the training. They were also instructed not to share these materials with their colleagues.

2. One or two days before each training session, project staff visited the institution in order to select two patient-defendants for demonstration interviews which were to be part of the training format. These patients were advised of the purpose of the interviews, consent forms were obtained and the Competency Screening Test was administered.

3. The actual training began with a demonstration interview by the principal investigator, after which all participants (roughly half of whom had not seen the CAI instrument before) were asked to score the CAI. (All demonstration interviews were videotaped.) All participants filled out questionnaires indicating discipline, previous experience with the competency issue, etc.

4. Following the initial demonstration interview, copies of the CAI *Handbook* were handed out and a discussion ensued designed to familiarize the trainees with the CAI *Handbook* and its use with particular reference to and discussion of the scoring of the initial demonstration patient.

5. Following the introduction to the CAI and usually in the afternoon of the first day, project staff provided further training with the following outlined content:
   a. Discussion of the new procedures and provision of the Massachusetts Mental Health Reform Act of 1970, as they apply to the competency issue;
   b. Brief history of the competency issue plus its significance:
      (1) number of persons affected
      (2) destructive effects of long-term criminal hospitalization.
   c. Data demonstrating the competency of the great major-

17

ity, even of the psychotic:
- (1) return to competency frequently within weeks to months of hospitalization
- (2) followup studies of psychotic offenders

d. Data demonstrating that the defendant and society are best served by a speedy trial or other disposition:
- (1) followup studies

e. "Dispositive" orientation of the courts and opportunities for more rehabilitative management of mentally ill defendants:
- (1) superiority of civil alternatives available under Massachusetts law, *nolle prosequi*, "filing," etc.
- (2) those flexible and constructive alternatives to full institutionalization of the incompetent or mentally ill defendant such as an alternative to prosecution, day hospital, night hospital programs, treatment as a condition of probation, etc.—all now possible under our new Mental Health Reform Act.

f. Protectionist bias of psychiatrists and its effects:
- (1) higher standards generally applied by psychiatrists than case law requires
- (2) therapeutic neglect of the criminally committed incompetent which calls for an active therapeutic investment—both a responsibility and an opportunity—in order to restore or increase competency
- (3) followup studies which demonstrate that in the absence of civil alternatives, a speedy completion of the criminal proceedings is the next best constructive disposition for the mentally ill defendant.

g. "Preventive detention" aspects and its risk:
- (1) exaggeration of the dangerousness of the mentally ill when they are also labeled criminal as in incompetency for trial findings
- (2) followup studies demonstrating the low level of criminal or dangerous recidivism in the group.

h. Importance of screening prior to mental hospital admission on the competency question:
- (1) data demonstrating the inappropriateness of the overwhelming majority of mental hospital admissions for competency workups
- (2) unnecessary stigmatization of the defendant, waste of professional manpower, and unnecessary expense in the absence of screening prior to admission.

i. Competency Screening Test:

18

(1) usefulness to screen out unnecessary mental hospital admissions

(2) adjunctive semiprojective data relative to competency determination is provided by the instrument

(3) demonstration of the scoring of the instrument using the initial demonstration patient.

6. Following the delivery of the training content outlined above, participants were dismissed and asked to return on the following morning for a second demonstration interview of a patient-defendant and the scoring of the CAI for the second or "graduation" time, again with an exercise in consensus-seeking. The technique of multiple-observer consensus-seeking was emphasized as a successful model which had led to the establishment of high interrater reliability by the project staff.

At this writing (June 15, 1972) favorable negotiations with the Massachusetts Defenders Committee (State supported defense attorneys for the indigent) and the Chief Justice of the District Court have led to the commitment of the two groups to a training exercise by project staff for the two groups. It is planned that we will use the training videotape edited from the 16 video-taped demonstrator patient-defendants of the above described training in order to prepare the lawyers and judges for the use of the CAI in particular (and the CST) in their courts. These training sessions are planned for the fall of 1972.

CHAPTER III

Methodology

A. Rationale

To be fit for trial, it is assumed that a person must have minimal affective and cognitive resources to assume the role of a defendant in court. Lacking these resources, the individual would be deprived of his due process right to testify in his own defense, confront witnesses against him, and to generally maintain an effective *presence* in court beyond his mere physical presence there. The issue of competency is thus an essentially legal issue, not a psychiatric issue. The criteria for competency to stand trial are concerned with the protection of the individual in the criminal system in order that he may be assured of a fair trial. Whether or not the person has physical or psychological defects is irrelevant except to the extent that it substantially interferes with fitness for trial.

The common law criteria for competency are defined as (1) an ability to cooperate with one's attorney in one's own defense; (2) an awareness and understanding of the nature and object of the proceedings; and (3) an understanding of the consequences of the proceedings. Within the framework of these criteria, a judgment must be made as to whether an accused person should stand trial without undue delay or whether the trial should be deferred until such time as the accused shall meet a minimal standard based on these criteria.

It is important that the assessment or evaluation of the defendant be made with a clear understanding of the requirements of the legal system. Psychological evaluation must be directed toward determining how well the individual will be able to meet the minimum requirements of the three common law criteria for competency. Issues such as criminal responsibility or the possibility of rehabilitation are not relevant considerations.

During the first year of the study, in the first stage of the development of the Competency Screening Test, samples from several populations were administered an early version of the test.

This procedure was designed to elicit a wide range of responses to the items in order to determine if there were differences in the responses as a result of the population backgrounds. Thus, the construction of a final instrument could be based on base-line data for comparative purposes. The groups that were administered this test included a group of persons civilly committed to a State hospital near Boston (other than Bridgewater); a men's church club (whose members approximated in socioeconomic backgrounds that of our Bridgewater samples); college undergraduates in a juvenile delinquency course; nonhospitalized defendants preparing for trial; and committed patients at Bridgewater who were in various stages of rehabilitation.

These first efforts at test construction provided the researchers with an initial opportunity to select and refine items that tended to elicit the most relevant responses for competency, while providing the opportunity to look at a range of responses from these various different populations. During the second and third years of the project, particular attention was given to two different samples of persons who had recently been sent to the Bridgewater State Hospital for observation to determine their competency to stand trial.

During the second year, one group of patients was selected on essentially a random basis to yield a representative sample of the general population of patients then committed to Bridgewater for 35-day competency observations. This group of 51 patients is known as the second year sample.

During the third year, the second sample was selected by psychiatric project staff out of the general competency population of Bridgewater then being observed. The 53 subjects who were deliberately screened into the research study were those who showed some type of psychosis or moderate or severe mental retardation. This was done because the representative second year sample contained very few persons about whom the issue of incompetency could be seriously raised. This high pathology group of 53 subjects was known as the third year sample.

Both the second and third year samples received not only the Competency Screening Test but also the full range of standard tests, the CAI, other new instruments, psychiatric interviews, and followup interviews and observations during and after subsequent court hearings. The following discussion briefly describes the major research procedures.

B. Development of Assessment Instruments

1. *General Procedure:* After the initial selection of subjects for the study, the psychological, legal, and psychiatric teams of the

project worked independently of each other, conducting separate interviews, test administration, and evaluation, without sharing the specific case data with each other. In this way, various modalities of competency were investigated independently and subsequently analyzed as variables not biased by the findings of the other investigators.

Within the first 2 weeks after referral to Bridgewater, the subjects were seen separately by the psychological and psychiatric teams. The legal team saw the subjects and their attorneys usually immediately after or within less than 2 weeks following a hearing on competency or trial on the merits or other legal actions.[1] The project investigators identified themselves, and indicated that they were from the university and that they were not connected with the courts or with Bridgewater. The investigators pointed out that they were trying to learn what happened to persons who were sent to Bridgewater in order to improve the situation. It was made clear that our work with them would not affect their case in any way and that strict confidentiality and privilege would be maintained. With very few exceptions, the subjects agreed to participate in the study.[2]

The psychiatric team used primarily the Competency Assessment Instrument (CAI) during their interviews with the patients. This instrument, based upon a structured interview, was aimed toward quantifying the criteria for competency based upon an assessment of the availability of appropriate courtroom behavior (see Appendix B).

The psychological tests were both traditional and new instruments. Standard forms of the Minnesota Multiphasic Personality Inventory (MMPI), the Graham Kendall Memory for Design Test, the Wechsler Adult Intelligence Scale (WAIS), the Rorschach, and the Draw-a-Person Test were administered. The new instruments developed were the Competency Assessment Instrument (CAI), the Courtroom Apperception Test (CRAT), the Make-believe Case, the Social Responsibility Test, and the Competency Screening Test (CST).[3] The general purpose of these instruments was to assess

---

1. Other legal actions in a few cases included dismissal of the original charges, a probable cause hearing, or additional observation at a State hospital. A few subjects and their attorneys were interviewed twice.

2. Occasionally, a very suspicious or aggressive individual would object to the testing. In such cases, he would be politely excused with the comment that he need not participate if he did not wish to do so. Over the 2-year period, this situation arose four or five times.

3. The Make-believe Case and the Social Responsibility Test were of an experimental nature. They attempted to investigate aspects of the subjects' attitudes related to social responsibility and concepts of justice and legal process. The results at this stage are impressionistic and would require further content analysis in order to establish whether these instruments have suitable reliability and validity.

those aspects of personality and functioning which were closely related to the legal criteria of competency. In addition, special followup protocols were designed to collect data during courtroom observations and followup interviews of the second and third year subject samples.

2. *Subjects:* The second year sample of 51 subjects was essentially randomly selected from the total population at Bridgewater currently committed for 35 days of competency observation.[4] This sample, which was generally representative of the larger Bridgewater population, was entirely male, 53.1 percent single, 77.5 percent unskilled laborers, 12.0 percent black, and had a mean educational level of tenth grade. The most frequent, alleged offenses were homicide, assault, larceny, and misdemeanors. A more detailed demographic description of the experimental samples and the total Bridgewater population can be obtained from the authors.

The third year sample of 53 subjects was specifically selected from the larger Bridgewater population on the basis of an indication of psychosis or mental retardation. This third year sample was also entirely male, 58.0 percent single, 28.0 percent unskilled laborers, 32.1 percent black, and had a mean educational level of tenth grade. Approximately 72.6 percent of this third year sample was given a diagnosis of some form of schizophrenia by Bridgewater. In contrast, 28.6 percent of the randomly selected second year sample were diagnosed by Bridgewater as having some form of schizophrenia.

The second and third year samples were extensively studied and tested. Data from these samples were used in the development of the interview protocol and test instruments described below.

3. *Competency Assessment Instrument (CAI):* This instrument (Appendix B) was designed to improve communication between the disciplines of `psychiatry and the law in the determination of competency to stand criminal trial. Prior attempts at such communication have suffered from the understandable tendency of each of the two disciplines to adhere to the language and concepts of their own discipline. Thus the clinical findings of the psychiatrist have not been delivered in a form and in language which are adequate for the needs of the court. Insofar as psychiatric opinion has been delivered to the court in this area, it has tended to be global, conclusional, and not substantiated by relevant clinical data. An effort was made, therefore, to develop an instrument which would deliver psychiatric opinion to the court in language, form, and

---

4. The total N of the second and third year samples varies on certain items of analysis because of some missing or incomplete data.

substance sufficiently common to both disciplines to provide a basis for adequate and relevant communication. The purpose of the instrument was to standardize, objectify, and quantify the relevant criteria for competency.

This instrument consists of a series of 13 functions related to an accused's ability to cope with the trial process in an adequately self-protective manner. These functions or items were culled from appellate cases, the legal literature, and our clinical and courtroom experience. The total series is intended to cover all possible grounds for a finding of incompetency. The weight which the court will assign to one or another of the items in its determination of competency will not be equal, nor is it intended to be. Neither will the weight assigned to a given item by the court in reaching a finding on competency for a particular defendant necessarily apply to the next defendant. For example, in the court's view it may be far more critical of the defense of a particular defendant that he be able to "testify relevantly" than for another defendant whose attorney does not intend to put him on the stand. Consideration of the weight to be assigned a given item in the case of a particular defendant goes beyond the scope of what should be expected of the examining psychiatrist. The task for the psychiatrist is that of providing objective data, the import of which is the responsibility of the court.

Each item is scaled from one to five, ranging from "total incapacity" at one to "no incapacity" at five.[5] A basic assumption is made in the scoring that the defendant will be adequately assisted by his attorney. The version of the CAI in Appendix B is the third major revision of this instrument. Earlier versions had grown to 15 items or functions but 2 of these items appeared to be duplicative and were dropped.

To determine the interrater reliability of the CAI, the second version of the instrument was statistically analyzed in the summer of 1970. Two raters independently scored the CAI for 16 patients on 18 different items[6] such as "understood procedure," "appreciation of charges," and "capacity to testify." Interrater correlations ranged from .895 on "legal strategy" to .09 on "unmanageable behavior." Correlations using standard Z scores were generally low with a mean of .63. It appeared that in general the raters were not consistent.

A further analysis using t-tests was conducted on the 18 items. This was done to determine whether the raters might have been

---

5. A score of 6 was used when the data did not permit a rating with reasonable certainty.

6. Eighteen items were scored because one of the items consisted of six sub-items.

consistent on scoring some items but inconsistent in scoring others through the use of different subjective base scores.[7] T-tests using the difference scores between the raters compared to a zero reference point produced only one item ("directions to counsel") that was statistically significant at the .05 level or less. The item "legal strategy" which had an interrater correlation of .895 had a p value of .055 and "appraisal of outcome," which had an interrater correlation of .890, had a p value of .055. All other items had either low interrater correlations (suggesting inconsistency) or t-tests that indicated that the raters were scoring at different levels.

Except for two or three items, the CAI did not at that stage of its development appear to meet the customary standards for reliability of test instruments. Therefore, scores of patients on the CAI were not used in the subsequent factor and discriminant analyses.

In an effort to tighten and sharpen the interrater reliability of the CAI, a definitional manual or *Handbook* (Appendix B) was developed which defined each of the items and contained a structured interview protocol and clinical examples of levels of incapacity corresponding to the graded scores. Also, the levels of functioning to be scored were reduced from six to five.

During the fall of 1971 and the spring of 1971 project activities returned to Bridgewater and Suffolk Superior Court with this final version of the CAI. Eighteen new subjects were examined by seven observers. The observers included three professionals previously inexperienced in the competency issue. Two were postgraduate psychiatrists who were community mental health fellows at the Laboratory of Community Psychiatry and the third was a lawyer-social worker. Frequent reference to the scoring manual (CAI Handbook) was resorted to during the examinations of the eighteen patient sample in seeking consensus and interrater reliability. In each case, however, the consensus seeking followed the scoring and the scores were left unchanged for purposes of subsequent statistical analysis of interrater reliability.

Because more than two observers rated each patient, it was possible to examine reliability using an intraclass correlation coefficient (R).[8] A group of three of the most experienced raters was compared with a group of the three least experienced raters at the conclusion of interviews with the total sample of patients. On the

---

7. For example, rater A may always score a certain type of response at 2 whereas rater B may always score this response at 4. This would produce a high correlation between the raters on the response but their levels of rating would be different.

8. The intraclass correlation formula used included systematic level differences between the raters as a part of error variance reducing correlation coefficients.

25

18 CAI items, correlation coefficients for the most experienced raters ranged from .84 to .97 with an average of .92. The least experienced raters produced correlation coefficients ranging from .43 to .96 with an average of .87. The least experienced raters, who generally rated five or more patients, showed a gradual increase in their average intraclass correlation coefficient from .64 to the final .87 as the number of patients they interviewed increased.

In this exercise, the discussions among raters following an interview provided immediate feedback in regard to the reliability of scores. The *Handbook* provided a consistent source of definitions and guidelines for resolving ambiguity. These two factors may have contributed much to the development of the high levels of reliability.

There were several additional strategies which were used to increase reliability: interviews were consistently structured to elicit information about each item in serial order, three or more judges were used to help overcome the bias or systematic errors of one judge, items were worded unambiguously, and all of the interviews were conducted in similar settings.

The high levels of reliability obtained with the CAI indicate that it is possible for clinical personnel to assess, over time, major characteristics related to competency to stand trial in a reliable manner. However, the extensive care and training involved in obtaining this reliability also cautions against assuming that satisfactory levels of reliability for rating scales can be obtained without considerable clinical use and evaluative feedback.

4. *Courtroom Apperception Test (CRAT)*: This projective test followed the same format as the Thematic Apperception Test. It was initially envisioned that this test would be used with individuals who had a writing or illiteracy problem and with those individuals whose responses were marginal or questionable on the other tests. The test was to sample perceptual rather than psychomotor responses.

Initially, 11 pictures directly and indirectly dealing with the criminal justice system were devised. The subject was told that the pictures dealt with courtroom scenes, and he was asked (1) to make up a story around a courtroom situation; (2) to say who the people were, what they were doing, and what the problem might be; and (3) to end the story. All responses were tape recorded.

A preliminary examination of the results from the 11 pictures suggested that their number should be reduced to 4 cards which were felt to deal more directly with the legal criteria for competency. A scoring system was devised that attempted to translate the response into legally-oriented scales. However, adequate interrater reliability could not be obtained for this test.

In retrospect, the poor performance of the Courtroom Apperception Test may be attributed to the use of too many scales for scoring each picture, especially in view of the concreteness and lack of elaboration so characteristic of our population. A single global rating of each picture might also avoid the high level of intercorrelation that appeared to exist among the initial scoring scales. To be useful, the test would require much further development.

5. *Competency Screening Test* (*CST*): The Competency Screening Test (Appendix A) was developed using a sentence completion format. The sentence completion method has a long history in psychological assessment and has been found to be a valuable clinical and research approach that compares favorably in economy and power with other psychiatric devices (Fiske and Van Buskirk 1959; Goldberg 1965; Rotter and Willerman 1947; Karen 1961). The sentence completion format involves the construction of a list of beginning phrases (or sentence stems) and the development of a rationale for coding the wide range of responses that a sentence stem may elicit. Typical stems included the following: "When Bob disagreed with his lawyer on his defense....," "When I think of being sent to prison....," and "If I had a chance to speak to the judge...." Administration of the final version of the CST takes about 15 minutes.

Beginning with 50 items, an early form of the CST was given to a wide range of competent and incompetent populations. The test was structured with the intent to focus on three kinds of items — those that represented the potential for a constructive relationship between the client and his lawyer, those that related to the client's understanding of the court process, and those that related to his ability to deal emotionally with the criminal process. On the basis of preliminary results, scoring techniques were defined and items that were not differentiating were eliminated.

The CST presently contains 22 items which are scored along integrated legal and psychological criteria. This produces a single score of 2 (competent), or 1 (questionable), or 0 (incompetent) on each of the 22 items. Adequate interrater reliability was easily obtained (with raters at a bachelors degree level) with a brief period of training. Interrater reliability using standard Z scores was .93. (A list of the 22 items and a scoring manual are contained in Appendix A.)

The next step in the analysis of the Competency Screening Test involved a factor analysis of its 22 individual items. The scores on these items obtained from the second and third year samples (N=91) were factor analyzed using a varimax orthogonal rotation.[9] Six rotated factors accounted for 56.3 percent of the total variance of the test (see table 1).

Factor 1 accounted for 19.5 percent of the common variance or communality explained by the six factors. This factor had the highest loading on items that clearly related to the dimension of the test that was intended to deal with the relationship of the defendant to his attorney in developing his defense. Factor 2, which accounted for 18.7 percent of the communality, showed the highest loading on those items that dealt with the defendant's understanding and awareness of the nature of the court process. Factor 3, which accounted for 18.8 percent of the communality, appeared to be parceling out that aspect of the defendant's responsiveness to the court process dealing with his reaction to accusation and guilt. This kind of responsiveness seems to deal with an affective or emotional level, in contrast to other aspects of competency that relate to cognitive capacities.

Factor 4, which accounted for 15.7 percent of the communality, included high loadings on items that could also be subsumed under the criterion of the defendant's understanding and awareness of the court process. However, some of the items with high loadings can also be interpreted as related to judgmental qualities in the defendant and to participation in strategic or evaluative requirements in playing the role of defendant in one's own trial.

Factor 5, which accounted for 11.5 percent of the communality, showed high loadings on only two items; these reflected the defendant's trust and confidence in his lawyer. Factor 6, which accounted for 15.5 percent of the communality, had substantial loadings on those items that indicate a future orientation. In this respect, it seems to be related to that criterion of competency that focuses on the seriousness of the circumstances in which the defendant finds himself, or the peril of his position. The appropriateness of the planfulness of the defendant seems to be reflected in this factor.

A separate factor analysis was then conducted using scores on the Competency Screening Test attained by a generally normal sample (N=83) containing no persons under observation for competency. The factor structure produced by this sample was markedly different from the factor structure produced by the Bridgewater

9. This rotation was based upon a set of factors whose original positions were determined by the Principle Components Factor Analysis program of the Data-Text System (Harvard Computing Center). The varimax rotation simplifies the columns of the factor matrix. The computing methods are based upon those suggested by Harman (1964). Standard "normalized" factor loadings were used in the rotations.

samples. The clusters of factors did not produce any readily discernable concepts related to competency. The Competency Screening Test may thus be sample specific and may not measure competency in terms of the factors described above for populations differing from those of Bridgewater or populations not actively involved in criminal justice systems.[10]

A further study of the Competency Screening Test was conducted using regression analyses, canonical correlations, and discriminant analyses with Bridgewater's recommendations regarding competency as the dependent or criterion variable. Regression analyses using various item scores, summed scores, and factor scores indicated five items that could be parsimoniously used to predict Bridgewater's findings. These five items were:

9. When the lawyer questioned his client in court, the client said
13. When the witness testifying against Harry gave incorrect evidence he
14. When Bob disagreed with his lawyer on his defense
19. When I think of being sent to prison
22. If I had a chance to speak to the judge

An examination of the factor matrix (table 1) shows that item 9 loads on factors 3, 4, and 6; item 13 on factor 4; item 14 on factor 1; item 19 on factor 2; and item 22 on factor 6. Thus the patterns of factors and their related items on the CST appear to be related to the legal criteria of competency.[11]

After the conceptual integrity of the items of the CST was established by these factor analyses and regression analyses, the five most salient items (indicated above) were entered into several discriminant analyses to determine their predictive value. Predictive value was quite high when compared with Bridgewater recommendations, court determinations, and lawyer ratings. The results are summarized in the following chapter.

C. Training

During the later training and implementation phase of the project, the training procedures were designed in part to permit us to determine whether the CAI alone, or the instrument plus the study of its *Handbook*, or the instrument plus the *Handbook* and training

---

10. Characteristics of the Bridgewater samples and the general Bridgewater competency population can be obtained by writing to the authors.

11. This analysis is not meant to imply that these five CST items are the only useful items. A different pattern of items might emerge as equally useful for practical purposes, depending upon the sequence of the entry of the items into regression analyses.

Table 1. Rotated Factor Loadings

Variable Description	Item No.	1	2	3	4	5	6
The lawyer told Bill that	1	.734*	.133	.262	.149	-.013	-.067
When I go to court the lawyer will	2	.668*	-.005	.192	-.006	-.144	.333
When I prepare to go to court with my lawyer	5	.567*	.440	-.009	.096	.131	.221
When the lawyer questioned his client in court	9	-.329	.016	.428*	.449*	.070	.461*
When Bob disagreed with his lawyer on his defense	14	.561*	.040	.010	.350	.302	-.037
If Ed's lawyers suggests that he plead guilty, he	16	.146	.069	-.055	.802*	.091	.071
What concerns Fred most about his lawyer	17	.077	.071	.092	.106	.810⁺	.256
If I had a chance to speak to the judge	22	.115	.428	.200	-.261	.237	.523*
Jack felt that the judge	3	.207	.060	.632*	.009	-.347	.190
The way a court trial is decided	7	-.046	.564*	.160	.056	.014	.155
If Jack had to try his own case, he	10	.026	.590*	.008	-.025	.412*	-.102
Each time the D.A. asked me a question	11	.180	.271	.234	.315	-.038	.299
While listening to the witness testifying against me	12	.406*	.085	.491*	.313	.187	.092
When the witness testifying against Harry gave incorrect evidence, he	13	.267	.240	.298	.447*	.278	-.184
When they say a man is innocent until proven guilty	18	.168	.397	.177	.513*	-.123	.104
When the jury hears my case, they will	21	.309	.069	.413*	-.061	.131	.319
When Phil was accused of the crime	4	-.060	.221	.728*	-.054	.233	-.034
If the jury finds me guilty, I	6	.343	.038	.569*	.216	-.019	.129
When the evidence in George's case was presented to the jury	8	.171	.593*	.328	.167	-.107	-.010
When I was formally accused of the crime, I thought to myself	15	.158	.025	.080	.037	.187	.694*
When I think of being sent to prison	19	.210	.646*	-.109	.235	.063	.231
When Phil thinks of what he is accused of	20	-.008	.355	.022	.263	-.170	.576*

described, or nothing short of the long term continued consensus-seeking technique which project staff had been required to resort to, could establish acceptable interrater reliability for the CAI. Built into the design were the questions of whether clinical experience with the competency issue or the discipline of the trainee had an effect on the reliability of his scoring of the demonstration patients when compared to the scoring of these patients by experienced staff of the project.

CHAPTER IV

Comprehensive Results, Validation, And Products of the Project

A. Standard Test Results

As previously noted, a wide variety of test instruments and interview protocols were used to assess the subject populations of the study.

Personality characteristics such as empathy-object relationship, hostility, bodily preoccupation, and dependency did not consistently show a clear relationship to Bridgewater recommendations and court determinations of competency. Also, intelligence as measured by the Wechsler Adult Intelligence Scale was not significantly related to competency.

The MMPI F scale (validity scale) was significantly related to competency in the second year sample but not in the third year sample. There is some indication (Brozek and Schiele 1948) that either stress in the patient's life or severe neurosis or psychosis may account for elevated scores on the F scale. Scores on the Draw-a-Person Test (female) tended toward showing a significant difference between competent and incompetent subjects in the third year sample. It is difficult to infer the meaning of this relationship. Because the test was scored as a measure of anxiety, it may be that the female subject matter produced a measured elevation of anxiety which is related to competency.

Scores on the Graham Kendall Memory for Design Test used as a measure of organic impairment were not significantly related to competency. However, these scores combined with scores from other tests may be helpful in selecting competent from incompetent persons.[1] Both the Graham Kendall and the Draw-a-Person Test are psychomotor tests at elemental levels, which is also a minimal requirement in terms of intactness in functioning on the Compe-

---

1. The use of combinations of scores from these standard tests and from specially developed tests to predict competency by discriminant analyses is discussed in the following section of this chapter.

tency Screening Test. If a subject is not able to take a pencil and articulate a fundamental task on paper, he is not able to meet this minimal requirement. Beyond this requirement, it has been found that severely disturbed persons frequently score high on the Graham Kendall.

Although there may be disturbed persons who are incompetent for trial, thus accounting for some correlation between tests of personality disorder and competency, there may also be many persons with severe pathology or mental illness requiring treatment who are nevertheless competent to stand trial. Thus it is possible that while personality tests and other tests of pathology may overlap with competency factors, there may be pathology in which competency is not an issue, for example, in some cases of paranoid schizophrenia.

B. Competency Screening Test

The initial study of the validity of the Competency Screening Test (CST) involved a comparison of summed scores on the CST with Bridgewater's recommendations regarding the competency of the subjects. This analysis employed a 2x2 format that would later be the format for more sensitive computer analyses. At the time of this analysis, 43 cases were available in the third year sample.[2] Based upon a clinical examination of the scores of this sample a cut-off point was selected (by PDL and DL) which dichotimized the sample into low (incompetent) and high (competent) scores. These scores were then compared with the competency recommendations made by Bridgewater. (Recommendations by Bridgewater are for all practical purposes identical with the court's decision and similar to attorney, opinions.)[3]

The relationship between the dichotimized scores on the Competency Screening Test and the disposition recommendations of the Bridgewater staff is indicated in table 2. Sixteen persons below the cutoff point were accurately predicted as incompetent and later indefinitely committed by the court as incompetent for trial. Out of 20 subjects scoring above the cutoff point on the CST

---

2. Third year cases were used because of the scarcity of incompetent cases in the second year sample.

3. Bridgewater recommendations of competency were identical with court judgments (no cases of disagreement) and closely related to attorney opinions of competency following a court hearing or trial ($x^2 =6.54$, 1 df., p=.01, Phi .59). This analysis which assumes statistical independence is not meant to imply that the determinations made by the psychiatrists, courts, and lawyers were in fact completely independent but that the determinations were made by separate categories of persons in the criminal justice system.

Table 2. Patients indefinitely committed or returned to
trial as a function of high and low scores on the
Competency Screening Test

Pretrial disposition	Competency Screening Test			
	Low		High	
Committed	Schizophrenic	15	Schizophrenic	3
	Mental deficiency	1		
		16		3 19
Returned to trial	Schizophrenic	2	Schizophrenic	7
	Mental deficiency	2	Antisocial behavior	2
	Antisocial behavior	1	Schizoid personality	3
	Schizoid personality	2	Toxic psychosis	2
			Personality disorder	2
			Chronic brain sydrome	1
		7		17 24
		23		20 43

(competent), 17 were later found to be competent by the court and returned to trial.

The predictive accuracy of the CST (agreement with subsequent court determinations of competency) can be further increased by weighting the score a subject receives on those items of the test that are most predictive. Factor analyses followed by regression analyses (Chapter III) indicated five items that were particularly predictive.[4] Using weighted scores on these items, a step-wise discriminant analysis was conducted with the third year Bridgewater sample.[5] All 16 patients who were later found competent by the court were also predicted as competent by the discriminant analysis as shown in table 3. However, three patients who were predicted as competent were found incompetent. The overall predictive accuracy of the CST was 89.7 percent.

4. These five items were:
9. When the lawyer questioned his client in court, the client said
13. When the witness testifying against Harry gave incorrect evidence, he
14. When Bob disagreed with his lawyer on his defense
19. When I think of being sent to prison
22. If I had a chance to speak to the judge
5. The step-wise discriminant analysis program (BMD07M) was written by Paul Sampson of the Health Sciences Computing Facility, UCLA. It is based upon a canonical correlation procedure (Rao 1962). The number of subjects in this third year sample was reduced to 29 for these discriminant analyses because of missing data for some of the subjects.

Predictive accuracy has been further increased by combining items from standard tests with the CST. A step-wise discriminant analysis using two standard test items (Graham Kendall and Draw-a-Person Test—female) and four CST items predicted competency findings with an overall accuracy of 93.1 percent as presented in table 4.[6]

The CST alone or in combination with other tests does not predict with complete accuracy the competency recommendations of Bridgewater or the competency determinations of the court (literally synonymous with Bridgewater recommendations). An analysis of the "misclassified" cases (those cases in which CST predictions differ from court determinations) suggests that mentally retarded persons may tend to be considered competent by Bridgewater and the court when in fact their fitness for trial in our opinion is uncertain. Alternatively, some persons may be committed as incompetent who are fit for trial because they have exhibited behavior which is particularly disturbing to the community. A closer examination of those cases with high scores who were

6. The six variables that best predicted competency were (1) Graham Kendall; (2) Draw-a-Person Test (female); (3) "When the lawyer questioned his client in court, the client said;" (4) "When Bob disagreed with his lawyer on his defense;" (5) "When I think of being sent to prison;" and (6) "If I had a chance to speak to the judge." The major contribution came from the CST items. Weights for raw scores for the six variables were -0.03 (G-K), -0.08 (DAP), 0.45 (Lawyer), -0.55 (Bob), 0.63 (Prison), 0.30 (Speak).

Table 3. Predictive accuracy of the Competency Screening Test
by discriminant analysis using Court Determinations of
Competency as the criterion variable

Court	Screening test	
	Competent	Incompetent
Competent	16	3
Incompetent	0	10

Table 4. Predictive accuracy of the Competency Screening Test
and Standard Test items by discriminant analysis using Court
Determinations of Competency as the criterion variable

Court	Screening test and test items	
	Competent	Incompetent
Competent	18	1
Incompetent	1	9

later committed as incompetent reveals that they tend to be persons who have a history of aggressive antisocial behavior and have deviated in a way that is especially repugnant to society.[7]

Followup studies in which patients and their attorneys were interviewed following court hearings revealed a high level of agreement between Bridgewater recommendations, court findings, and CST predictions. Global ratings by attorneys as to whether they considered their defendants competent or incompetent were significantly related to both CST scores[8] and court determinations of competency.[9] Although the attorneys were aware of the court determinations at the time of their rating, they were not aware of the CST scores previously received by their defendants. Thus, in this initial study, the CST appears to measure with reasonable accuracy the competency of defendants within the Massachusetts criminal justice system.

C. Demonstration and Validation of the Competency Assessment Instrument and the Competency Screening Test

It had been our plan during the fourth year of the originally scheduled 5 years of this grant, to bring our team and instruments into actual competency proceedings in the courts of Massachusetts. An opportunity arose in the spring of 1970 to proceed with a limited demonstration. Fifteen legal actions were brought concerning men who had been committed to Bridgewater as incompetent to stand trial and whose commitments were defective in relation to the Rohrer decision of the Massachusetts Supreme Judicial Court (Robey 1965). A third year psychiatric resident from Boston University Medical School on an elective traineeship with us and the Medical Director of Bridgewater were given access to the Competency Assessment Instrument (CAI) in the preparation of their testimony on the competency issue in these hearings. In addition, the Competency Screening Test was given to the 15 defendants but its results were kept blind and independent of the CAI scoring.

Justice Alan Hale of the Massachusetts Superior Court presided at the hearings and welcomed the use of the CAI in the cases and the

---

7. One case involved the murder by the patient of his child and one involved a sexual assault on a child. The third case involved disturbing the peace, a relatively nonserious offense from a legal point of view; however, this disturbance involved a threat to kill a police officer.

8. Fisher Exact Test = 0.02; phi = 0.61.

9. Fisher Exact Test = 0.02; phi = 0.59.

instrument was the basis of the expert testimony on the competency issue. Justice Hale made frequent reference to the instrument in his examination of the issue and expressed his satisfaction with its usefulness. The instrument was accepted into evidence in each case. The Judge's findings proved to be consistent with the CAI ratings and the Competency Screening Test in all but one case for each instrument.[10]

This limited demonstration hardly suffices to establish the validity of these two instruments, particularly since an earlier form (version two) of the CAI was used. However, the feasibility and practicality of the use of the CAI in competency hearings appears to have been established reasonably well. Clearly the instrument provided a basis for relevant and adequate interdisciplinary communication on the issue of competency to stand trial in these hearings.

Added to the Rohrer hearings was the earlier Dennis Ford workup which was accepted into evidence by Chief Justice Tauro, then of the Superior Court, in a borderline case which had already received several inconclusive hearings on the competency issue. This competency evaluation, which was prepared by the project staff, described the CAI and Competency Screening Test in detail with verbatim quotations from the patient-defendant substantiating the ratings. Chief Justice Tauro accepted this evaluation into evidence and based his finding of the patient-defendant's incompetency on the written evaluation and the testimony of one of the project psychiatrists which was based on the CAI.

Although the interrater reliability of the CAI has now been demonstrated, its validity remains to be adequately established. This can be done only in the courtroom. In our experimental sample, there has been an excellent fit between Bridgewater's findings, the independently scored CAI, the Competency Screening Test, and the posthearing ratings by defense counsel of the performance of defendants. But three of these rating variables (other than the Competency Screening Test) are not completely independent. The Bridgewater staff has been influenced by our work although they were not directly aware of our findings in the

---

10. The judge found one defendant competent although he scored low on several of the CAI items. In this case the low scores arose from a claimed amnesia on the part of the defendant who may have been malingering. On this defendant the CST scores were in the competent range.

On a second defendant who scored in the competent range on the CST both the CAI and the judge found him to be incompetent. This patient, during the hearing before the judge, audibly responded to auditory hallucinations.

Applying the Fisher's Exact Probability Test to the above data indicates that the observed distribution of the scores of the CST had a one-tailed probability of occurrence of $p < .005$.

experimental sample. The attorneys have been influenced by the Bridgewater findings, and the courts tend to be uncritical of the Bridgewater findings. It is nevertheless encouraging that Bridgewater found only 15 out of 476 men to be incompetent in 1970 and only 6 out of 501 in 1971. This is quite consistent with our own base rate estimates.

Other methods of establishing validity by moot courts or groups of judges or distinguished defense counsel serving as independent raters were considered by us but were not carried through by reason of impracticality and expense.

D. Published Papers Arising in Whole or Part from the Project

1. Balcanoff, E.J. and McGarry, A.L. Amicus curiae: The role of the psychiatrist in pretrial examinations. *Amer J Psychiat*, 126:342-347, 1969.

2. Balcanoff, E.J. The psychiatrist in a Superior Court setting. *Mental Hygiene*, 55:45-50, 1971.

3. Bendt, R.H.; Balcanoff, E.J.; and Tragellis, G.S. Psychiatric examination of alleged offenders. *Amer Bar Assoc J*, 58:371-373, 1972.

4. Lipsitt, P.D. The dilemma of competency for trial and mental illness. *New Eng J Med*, 282:797-798, 1970.

5. Lipsitt, P.D.; Lelos, D.; and McGarry, A.L. Competency for trial: A screening instrument. *Amer J Psychiat*, 128:105-109, 1971.

6. McGarry, A.L.; Curran, W.J.; and Kenefick, D. Problems of public consultation in medico-legal matters: A symposium. *Amer J Psychiat*, 125:42-59, 1968.

7. McGarry, A.L., and Bendt, R.H. Criminal vs. civil commitment of psychotic offenders: A seven year follow-up. *Amer J Psychiat*, 125:1387-1393, 1969.

8. McGarry, A.L. Demonstration and research in competency to stand trial and mental illness: Review and preview. *Boston Univ Law Rev*, 49:1969.

9. McGarry, A.L. The fate of psychotic offenders returned for trial. *Amer J Psychiat*, 127:1181-1184, 1971.

10. McGarry, A.L. Titicut follies revisited: A long-range plan for the mentally disordered offender in Massachusetts. *Mental Hygiene*, 54:20-27, 1970.

11. Rosenberg, A.H. Competency for trial: A problem of interdisciplinary communication. *Judicature*, 53:316-321, 1970.

12. Rosenberg, A.H. Competency for trial: Who knows best? *Crim Law Bul*, Vol. 6, No. 11, 1970.
13. Rosenberg, A.H., and McGarry, A.L. Competency for trial: The making of an expert. *Amer J Psychiat*, 128:1092-1096, 1972.

E. Papers and Studies Arising in Whole or in Part from the Project but Not Yet Published

1. Bender, F. "Statutory and Case Law Survey on Competency To Stand Trial."
2. Lipsitt, P.D. "Competency: An Illustrative Example of a Psychological Task in the Legal Process."
3. McGarry, A.L., and Schwitzgebel, R.K. "Inter-rater Reliability and a New Instrument." Read at the Annual Meeting of the American Psychiatric Association, Dallas, Texas, May 4, 1972.
4. Rosenberg, A.H. "Massachusetts Statutory and Case Law on Competency To Stand Trial."
5. Rosenberg, A.H. "Competency for Trial: Observations of Court Practice in Massachusetts Courts."

F. Training Activities and Their Evaluation[11]

A total of 216 trainees from various disciplines (see table 5) participated in eight separate training sessions of one and one-half days each. A randomly selected group of trainees were sent a copy of the Competency to Stand Trial Assessment Instrument (CAI) with its *Handbook* approximately 1 week prior to the training session. At the training session, there was a brief introductory discussion of the purpose of the training and then an interview with the first patient who was rated by all the trainees on the CAI. Following this, there was a discussion of the rating and general discussion. On the second day, there was the presentation and rating of the second patient on the CAI. All of the interviews were structured around the items on the CAI and were conducted by the principal investigator.

The interrater reliability (agreement) among the trainees and trainers was evaluated primarily through the use of the intraclass R (see table 6). The intraclass R of the trainees on all of the 13 patients rated on the CAI was .84. The trainers had an intraclass R

---

11. A more detailed discussion of training methods and results can be found in Appendix C, "Evaluation of the Training Program."

Table 5. Background characteristics of trainees[a]

Characteristic		Percentage
Sex	Male	65.4
	Female	34.6
Age	21–30	29.9
	31–40	25.0
	41–50	24.5
	51–60	17.4
	61–70	3.2
Education	High School	1.6
	Some College	6.4
	B.A. or equivalent	19.1
	M.A. or equivalent	20.6
	M.D., Ph.D.	51.8
	Unknown	0.5
Discipline	Psychiatry	48.4
	Social Work	23.7
	Psychology	11.6
	Nursing	12.6
	Law	0.5
	Unknown	3.1
Examinations	None	43.1
	1–10	18.1
	11–50	18.6
	51–100+	20.2

[a]N=216

of .89 on all patients. The mere reading of the *Handbook* alone did not seem to influence the interrater reliability. Trainees both with and without the *Handbook* prior to the training obtained similar reliability (see table 6).

Following training, the reliability declined for trainees as well as the trainers — probably because of the specific characteristics of the patients interviewed (see table 6). The trainees with the *Handbook* prior to training had considerably higher reliability following training (R of .85) than the trainees without the *Handbook* (R of .72). An examination of the mean total scores of several subgroups of trainees suggests that the training had a differential impact on trainees with varying amounts of prior experience with competency examinations (see table 7). Following training, the trainees with very little or no prior experience or very much experience tended to

**Table 6. Intraclass R's for trainers and trainees
before and after training[a]**

Group	Before training	After training
Trainers	.90	.86
All Trainees[b]	.88	.78
Trainees without Handbook[c]	.87	.72
Trainees with Handbook[d]	.87	.85

[a]Caution should be used in interpreting R's based upon the small N of 3 raters and the 6 to 7 patients used in the various sub-samples here. At best, only very general patterns of agreement can be inferred from a comparison of the various intraclass R's.

[b]Trainees were randomly selected from all trainees.

[c]Trainees were randomly selected from only those trainees who had not received a *handbook* prior to training.

[d]Trainees were randomly selected from only those trainees who had received a *Handbook* prior to training.

Table 7. Mean total scores on CAI

Group	Before training	After training
Trainers	67.7	70.6
All Trainees	68.6	69.6
0-30 minutes of reading[a]		
No prior examinations[b]	67.7	72.3
1-10 examinations	58.8	73.7
11-50 examinations	68.8	76.7
51-100+ examinations	68.5	70.8
31 minutes-1 hour of reading		
No prior examinations	72.4	56.8
1-10 examinations	74.0	74.3
11-50 examinations	72.0	75.3
51-100+ examinations	62.0	73.4
1 hour or more of reading		
No prior examinations	67.8	53.3
1-10 examinations	76.0	69.8
11-50 examinations	78.5	61.3
51-100+ examinations	66.8	59.1

[a]Time spent reading the CAI *Handbook* prior to training.

[b]Number of competency examinations in which the trainee participated prior to training.

give ratings which were more divergent from the trainers' ratings than before training. There was also a trend for those trainees who spent 1 hour or more reading the *Handbook* to rate the patients as more incompetent than those trainees who spent less time reading the *Handbook*.

Generally, the training does not appear to have been successful. Future training should perhaps involve the feedback of ratings on the CAI to the trainees and a seeking of consensus on these ratings over an extended series of patients. This method was successfully used to establish a high level of reliability among the trainers.

In conclusion, however, it appears that the use of the CAI with interviews structured around its 18 items can produce satisfactorily high interrater reliability without extensive training. The *Handbook* seems to be helpful but may cause some trainees with little prior experience to perceive more incompetency than actually present.

G. Current Use of Competency Instruments (1972)

Two complementary inquiries were conducted in the spring of 1972 following our training activities in order to assess the utility and implementation of the Competency Screening Test and the Competency to Stand Trial Assessment Instrument.

The first followup involved a questionnaire mailed to those individuals requesting the Competency Screening Test. The second inquiry involved contacting all the Massachusetts State Hospitals participating in the competency training program.

A total of 115 requests for the CST were received from outside the State of Massachusetts, including 8 from foreign countries (see table 8). Over 50 percent of these inquiries originated in mental hospitals currently involved in competency evaluations. Medical schools followed the State Hospitals in frequency of request.

Responses to a followup questionnaire were received from 25 percent (N=27) of the original request population (see table 8). An analysis of these responses indicates that 11 institutions are not now using the instrument because of (1) procedural difficulties, (2) administrative obstacles, (3) resistance from the local courts and prosecutors, and (4) the varying standards of competency in different states.

The remaining respondents presently using the instrument are doing so in the following categories: (1) clinical evaluations, (2) research studies, (3) training of forensic psychiatrists, and (4) as part of academic courses.

Table 8. Requests for competency screening test

Source	Number of requests
UNITED STATES	
Hospitals and Mental Health Centers	52
Universities	
a. Psychology Departments	9
b. Medical Schools	10
c. Law Schools	3
Departments of Mental Health	7
Departments of Corrections	4
Court Clinics	4
Police Departments	1
Probation Officers	1
Prosecutors	1
Defense Attorneys	1
American Psychological Association	1
National Institute of Health	1
Miscellaneous	12
TOTAL U.S.A. Requests	107[a]
FOREIGN	
Hospitals and Mental Health Centers	5
Universities	2
Miscellaneous	1
TOTAL Foreign Requests	8
TOTAL Requests for CST Materials	115

[a]Number of followup letters sent from Laboratory of Community Psychiatry.

Table 9. Responses to followup letter

Source	Number of responses
Hospitals and Mental Health Centers	15
Universities	
a. Psychology Departments	5
b. Law Schools	1
Court Clinics	2
Departments of Mental Health	2
Police	1
Prosecutor	1
TOTAL responses	27

The second followup investigated the use of the Competency Screening Test and the Competency Assessment Instrument in the various Massachusetts State hospitals which were the sites of the training program.

All of these hospitals reported using the CST routinely in all competency cases referred from the court. Interestingly enough, Bridgewater State Hospital has recently instituted an administrative change whereby nurses, trained during the competency study, now administer and score the CST as part of every competency evaluation. The test and its results are subsequently incorporated into the patient's hospital record.

The Competency Assessment Instrument is reported as currently in use in all the State Hospitals except one which claimed that court requests for evaluations of competency were now rare events in that region of the State.

CHAPTER V

Significant Work by Others in the Area of Competency to Stand Trial

A. Check Lists

There have been several attempts by others to develop a "check list" for psychiatrists in their examination for competency other than our CAI (Robey 1965; Bukataman 1971).[1] None of these provides for quantification or graded degrees of incapacity. According to Robey, whose checklist was published in 1965, he has distributed some 2,600 copies of his check list and has "received and granted over 50 requests to republish it by Bar Associations, prosecuting attorneys' offices, etc., from many states, as well as from persons in England, Australia and Canada."[2] This would certainly suggest that there is an appetite for greater clarity and comprehensiveness in competency determinations. Aside from the lack of quantification in Robey's check list (there is a single column with the letters OK on the top), it appears to be legalistic and complex to an impractical degree. For example, the check list calls for a "psychiatric evaluation of court's expectations, if possible" in the area of defendant's "comprehension of court proceedings." In addition, Robey gives a prominent place in his check list to "susceptibility to decompensation while awaiting or standing trial." This would appear to be fraught with difficulty. The *prediction* of psychiatric decompensation is a very uncertain science and would seem to be inadequate grounds for denying the right to a speedy trial.

Bukataman and his associates (1971) recently published a check list for competency. This is a similar formulation to our CAI. It lacks quantification, and in our view is not exhaustive of valid bases for an incompetency finding. For example, there is no provision for the

---

1. Personal communication, Prof. Norval Morris, University of Chicago Law School, Center for Studies of Criminal Justice.

2. Personal communication, A. Robey, Nov. 2, 1970, Center for Forensic Psychiatry, Michigan Dept. of Mental Health, Ann Arbor, Michigan.

defendant who from a psychotic sense of guilt is motivated to irrationally seek punishment and work towards his own conviction. This is, to be sure, a relatively rare consideration.

The Illinois formulation[1] has a good deal of merit but again lacks quantification and includes much broader and less precise data than the narrow issue of competency calls for. This would appear to invite dispositional and other considerations which might cloud the competency issue.

B. The Judicial Conference of the District of Columbia

The Judicial Conference of the District of Columbia Circuit (1966) produced an excellent analysis of procedural and substantive issues related to competency determinations in the District. The report also contains extensive statistical data of pretrial examinations in the District of Columbia covering the years from 1952 through 1963 in the District (felony) Court. Similar to Massachusetts, the issue of competency appears to have been raised far too frequently in the District (3 out of every 10 prosecutions), and rates of incompetency findings appear to have been far too high, although in more recent years they have dropped significantly. Unlike our experience in Massachusetts, however, the length of hospitalization for committed incompetents in the District appears to have been far shorter.

C. The American Bar Foundation

Under the editorship of Matthews (1970), the American Bar Foundation has recently published *Mental Disability and the Criminal Law*. This work concerns itself largely with procedural and strategic considerations of the competency and criminal responsibility issues, and is highly consistent with our own observations and speculations. The use of competency procedures as a device for disposition seeking and strategic manipulation is well described in this work. It suffers, however, from a lack of hard data and documentation. The author elected to pursue a research model of "composite description."

46

CHAPTER VI

By-products and Relevant Accompaniments to the Research

A. Introduction

Research never takes place in a vacuum, particularly when it involves people. Although the design of this project, except for a truncated demonstration phase in 1969, called for the independent collection of research data, we have not been silent about our general findings and some of our work has already been published. It is not altogether surprising, therefore, that changes in the two great interfacing systems, that of mental health and criminal justice, have taken place in Massachusetts during our research, some of which is directly attributable to this project, some indirectly, and some not at all. The exhaustive documentation of such attribution would accomplish little beyond a self-serving purpose, but it is our responsibility to describe these changes and note our involvement in them. Such a description is complicated by the fact that members of the research team wear other hats in these systems. Project staff have served on a number of legislative and gubernatorial commissions during the years of our research activity and have been involved in appellate and legislative activities, some of which had a direct influence on the handling of the competency issue in Massachusetts. Obviously what was learned in the project about the issue became part of the contributions of project staff in these ancillary activities.

What follows is a description of clinical, administrative, appellate, and legislative activities on which the work of the project has directly or indirectly been brought to bear. It may be that the timing of the project was fortuitous and that some or much of what has changed during these years would have happened anyway.

B. "The Mental Health Reform Act of 1970," Chapter 888 of the *Acts of 1970, Commonwealth of Massachusetts,* as Amended by Chapter 470, *Acts 1971* (now Chapter 123 of the *General Laws of Massachusetts*)

Sections of this new mental health and retardation code enacted on September 1, 1970, relevant to competency procedures arose directly from the work of this project. They were drafted in large measure by the principal investigator (*Mass. G.L.* Chapter 123 Sections 15, 16, 17). His involvement in this recodification goes back to 1964 when the legal and field research which led to the legislation was under the directorship of the co-principal investigator under the auspices of the Special Commission on Mental Health of the Massachusetts Legislature. In the latter stages of the many drafts of the code and its several journeys through the legislature, the principal investigator directed the drafting in collaboration with legal counsel from the Office of the Governor. The statutory language represents the end product of a series of compromises arrived at in the legislative process and by reason of relevant appellate cases which came down from the U.S. Supreme Court during the years of the research for and redrafting of the new code.[1] Since these sections represent a series of compromises they do not perfectly reflect our views. In particular, an earlier provision whereby attorneys or "legal advisors" would have had an independent role from clinicians in the periodic review of the competency of committed pretrial incompetents, is no longer present. Earlier drafts more adequately represented our thinking on this issue (see Senate 941 of the legislative matters brought before the General Court of Massachusetts in 1968). We had declined to compromise on the issue in 1968 and partly for this reason that bill went down in defeat. Key legislators refused to add these "legal advisors" to "the fastest growing empire in the State," the Massachusetts Defenders Committee. In order to accomplish the passage of this code, with its reforms in many other areas, we decided to delete the "legal advisors" provision and elected to pursue this issue separately on its own merits without sacrificing the rest of the code. To date (June 15, 1972) the Massachusetts legislature has declined to establish a "legal advisors" program for the mentally ill.

The currently enacted sections of the code relevant to competency for trial became effective in Massachusetts on November 1, 1971. At this writing (June 15, 1972) statistics for the first 6

---

1. Notably from the United States Supreme Court, Baxstrom v. Herold (see footnote 8, page 60) and Pate v. Robinson (see footnote 2, page 2), and from the Massachusetts Supreme Judicial Court, Petition of Rohrer (see footnote 5, page 14) and Commonwealth v. Druken (see footnote 3, page 54).

months under the new Act were available (November 1971–April 1972). Based upon these statistics the impact of the new statute has been striking, particularly as it has affected competency for trial proceedings (see table 10 and figure 1). Projecting from the first 6 months data, there will be 1,044 fewer competency for trial admissions to Massachusetts Mental Hospitals during the first year under the new Act (there were 427 such admissions during the first 6 months compared to 949 during the corresponding 6 months the year before). These admissions include 110 pretrial admissions to Bridgewater during the first 6 months under the new Act as compared to 242 during the same period the year before.

Since the number of pretrial admissions actually declined during the second quarter-year under the new Act as compared to the first 3 months (198 compared to 228), it is not likely that these decreases are due to lack of familiarity with the new procedures. It is likely that the decline in pretrial admissions is largely attributable to the psychiatric screening examinations required under the new Act. Clearly, many hundreds of unnecessary admissions are being avoided under the new proceedings and this of course is consistent with the research findings of this project.

In addition to the decline in pretrial admissions for observation as noted above, there appears to be a decline in the number of prolonged commitments arising out of these observational admissions on the basis of a finding of incompetency for trial. Thus, during the first six months, only 20 such commitments eventuated. Projected to 40 for the first year, this represents a decline from 76 such commitments during fiscal year 1971, the last complete year before the new Act (see Figure 2). This would appear to be consistent with the base expectancy for accurately assessed incompetency findings that we would expect based on our research.

C. Intercurrent Statistical Changes at Bridgewater, Boston State Hospital and Throughout Massachusetts Prior to the Enactment of the Mental Health Reform Act of 1970

The principal field activities of this project took place at the State Hospital at Bridgewater (Department of Correction), and at the Boston State Hospital (Department of Mental Health). Although, in pursuing the activities of the project, we did not initially set out to educate and consult with the clinicians in these hospitals, and although we designed the research phases of the grant so that the data were not available to the clinicians, striking intercurrent changes took place in the handling of the competency issue particularly in these two institutions. As noted, we have not been

Table 10. Incompetency for trial admissions in Massachusetts
(General Laws, Chapter 123, Section 100)

Year	Sec. 100 Bridgewater Obs.	Sec. 100 Bridgewater Committed	Sec. 100 15 D.M.H. Hospitals Obs.	Sec. 100 15 D.M.H. Hospitals Committed	Total Observational Admissions	Total Prolonged Pretrial Commitments	All Admissions Bridgewater	All Admissions 15 D.M.H. Hospitals
					Fiscal Years			
1959	128	16	926	172	1054	188	255	10598
1960	129	27	876	172	1005	199	265	11061
1961	163	44	928	202	1091	246	286	11169
1962	214	47	983	197	1197	244	348	11637
1963	239	46	1122	247	1361	293	375	12306
1964	240	53	1245	223	1485	276	436	12319
1965	245	41	1231	172	1476	213	451	12573
1966	282	56	1307	203	1589	259	469	12326
1967	274	34	1325	240	1599	274	430	13479
1968	345	28	1393	128	1738	156	548	14121
1969	421	37	1488	147	1909	184	588	14803
1970	476	16	1625	127	2101	143	680	14114
1971	501	12	1387	62	1888	74	703	14237

Admissions during first 6 months under the New Mental Health Act and projections for the first year (General Laws, Chapter 123, Sections 15, 16, and 17, Effective November 1, 1971.)

Year	Sec. 100 Bridgewater Obs.	Sec. 100 Bridgewater Committed	Sec. 100 15 D.M.H. Hospitals Obs.	Sec. 100 15 D.M.H. Hospitals Committed	Total Observational Admissions	Total Prolonged Pretrial Commitments	All Admissions Bridgewater	All Admissions 15 D.M.H. Hospitals
11/71 to 4/72	110	6	317	14	427	20	218	6555
Projected First Year	220	12	634	28	854	40	436	13110

50

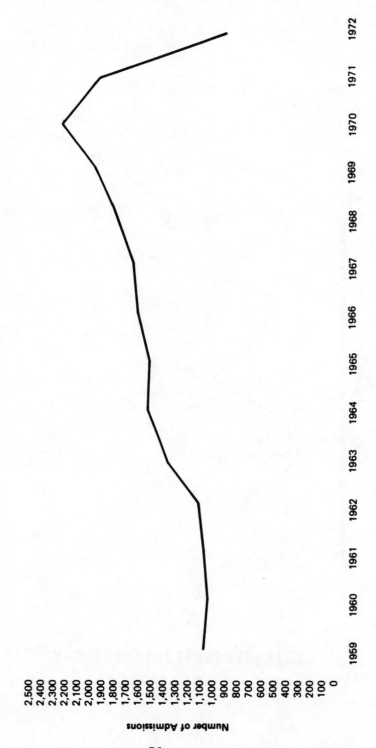

Figure 1

Incompetency for Trial (Observational) Admissions in Massachusetts

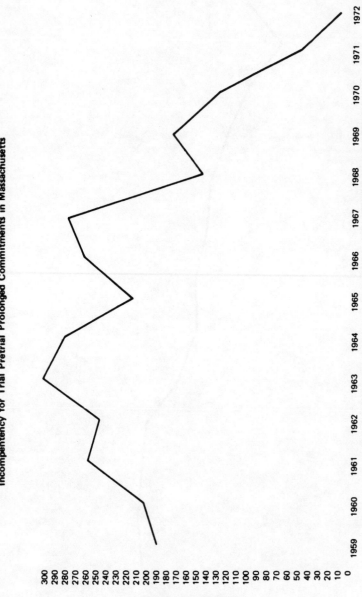

Figure 2

Incompentency for Trial Pretrial Prolonged Commitments in Massachusetts

Number of Commitments

Projected figure based on first six months under the new Mental Health Reform Act.

52

silent about our work and a number of our papers were published during the research phase of the project. It is not our intention to try to demonstrate that there is a cause and effect relationship between this project and these changes since many other factors were at work, but there is little question that there has been an impact.

Out of 163 observational admissions at Bridgewater in 1961, 36 (22.2 percent) were found to be incompetent to stand trial. Last year (FY71) Bridgewater committed only 6 (1.2 percent) out of 501 (see table 10 and figures 1 and 2). At Boston State in 1963, 27 (12.2 percent) were committed as incompetent. In 1970 only *one* person was committed out of 186 observational admissions.[2] In 1971 Boston State committed 4 (2.4 percent) out of 167.

Throughout the State the word had clearly gotten around to avoid indefinite pretrial commitments. Thus the rate of observational commitments declined from a high in 1963 of 293 (21.6 percent) out of 1,361 to 126 (6.0 percent) out of 2,101 by 1970. The sharp deline in incompetency commitment rates in FY 1970 is partly attributable to the impetus of the *Druken* decision (discussed below) of the Massachusetts Supreme Judicial Court, which came down in December of 1969.

The sharp increase in the numbers of defendants being sent by the courts for pretrial observational admissions prior to the new Act was disturbing. Clearly, the courts of the Commonwealth were casting a wider and wider net and catching fewer and fewer incompetents. Undoubtedly there were many factors which account for this. Massachusetts' recently liberalized bail laws may have created a pressure for "preventive detention" under the competency rubric. Such a suggestion is somewhat supported by the fact that the greatest increase in the numbers of competency admissions were at Bridgewater (from 270 in 1967 to 501 in FY 1971) which provides maximum security. Other facilities of this State in the Department of Mental Health, which offer minimal provisions for security, increased proportionately much less. As noted above in Section B, with adequate courthouse screening examinations, many hundreds of these stigmatizing and expensive admissions are

---

2. Dr. Robert Kaplan, the assistant superintendent, reports to us that consistent with our consultative and educative input to that institution in recent years (in which we wore several hats) their policy is to avoid pretrial incompetency commitments either by (1) promptly returning men for trial if they are competent, or (2) asking for short term extensions of the observational phase of the admissions so that they can actively treat such individuals and restore them to a maximum state of competency without indefinite commitment under criminal sanctions, or (3) actively negotiating with the courts to arrange for civil commitment with the criminal charges dropped when longer term hospitalization is required.

currently being avoided. It is anticipated that when the new instruments, particularly the CAI and Competency Screening Test, are more effectively introduced into the criminal justice system, many more of these unnecessary and destructive admissions can be prevented.

D. The *Druken* Decision of the Supreme Judicial Court of Massachusetts, 1969[3]

Joseph Druken was one of the third year sample. In the course of following Mr. Druken back to his competency hearing at the Roxbury District Court, a research attorney and a research psychiatrist from the project spent the better part of 2 days with the defense counsel for Mr. Druken in both formal (the attorney posttrial protocol) and informal contact. Defense counsel, from the Massachusetts Defenders Committee (Public Defenders) became sufficiently disturbed by the relative lack of legal and procedural safeguards in the commitment of Druken as incompetent for trial that he elected to appeal the commitment. The appeal was carried to the Supreme Judicial Court by the appellate division of the Massachusetts Defenders Committee. They argued that since commitment awaiting trial is a *civil* commitment all of the safeguards applicable to civil commitment should apply to commitment awaiting trial. The principal safeguard at that time which had not been accorded individuals committed and awaiting trial, in contrast to persons civilly committed without outstanding criminal charges, was the two-physician examination and certification by physicians not attached to the institution to which the person was being committed.

In this decision, which was delivered on December 22, 1969, the Supreme Judicial Court agreed with the arguments of the Massachusetts Defenders. Although the decision is somewhat ambiguous and in places naive,[4] it unequivocally established that the full panoply of civil safeguards are required for defendants who are to be committed as incompetent to stand trial.

It is too early to assess the full and long range impact of the Druken decision. As will be described below, it has already had a striking impact on the 496 defendants who were committed to the hospitals of the Department of Mental Health at the time this

---

3. Commonwealth v. Druken, 254 N.E. 2nd 779 (1970).

4. The decision states in part "The Superintendant of the Hospital, or the Commissioner of Mental Health and medical director dispose of the question of competency to stand trial in their report that a prisoner is insane." Here again we have the fallacy of equating "insanity" or mental illness with incompetency.

decision was delivered. This decision makes pretrial commitment procedurally much more complex than in the past when it was relatively simple and efficient (and unconstitutional) to commit such individuals under criminal procedure with criminal charges ostensibly still outstanding. It is likely that the courts will move increasingly toward using less complex civil and voluntary procedures for admission, which are now much easier to invoke, and dispose of the criminal charges. This will be particularly true of defendants accused of misdemeanors. These comprise about 80 percent of the total pretrial commitment group in Massachusetts. In short, there is reason to hope that the Druken decision is likely to help to decriminalize the management of most mentally ill alleged offenders in Massachusetts. Indeed, this already appears to be happening. As has been noted, in fiscal 1970 only *one* out of 186 patient-defendants was committed at Boston State Hospital with his charges still outstanding.

When the *Druken* decision came down, the legal counsel of the Department of Mental Health made the interpretation that the Department was required to apply the requirements of that decision *retroactively* to the patient-defendants who had been committed and were awaiting trial in the facilities of the Department of Mental Health. Patient-defendants at Bridgewater in the Department of Correction had already been judicially reviewed under the Baxstrom and Rohrer decisions and in large measure had their criminal status dissolved, (see below). During the spring of 1970 the legal office proceeded to survey the committed patient-defendants in Massachusetts mental health facilities other than Bridgewater. As of May 1, 1970, there were 496 persons awaiting trial in Department of Mental Health institutions in the status of indefinite commitment.

The next step the legal office elected to take was to survey the 60 courts in the Commonwealth where these commitments had originated. It was astonishing to learn that over 90 percent of the criminal charges against these patient-defendants were no longer outstanding. In 12 cases, the court had "no record" of any charges or their disposition. By the fall of 1970 only 46 still had active criminal charges out of 496 committed patients who were "awaiting trial." One hundred and seventy-six of these patients had been hospitalized more than 5 years, in a criminal status, without home visit privileges, for charges that for the most part no longer existed. One of our hospitals (Metropolitan State) promptly discharged 30 of these patients. As of May 1, 1970, 108 of the group of 496 had gone home. Others have remained but in a voluntary or civil status.

During this project, we had come across one court which "routinely" dismissed the charges while *at the same time* committing defendants indefinitely awaiting trial. We were not prepared for the remarkable fact that 212 out of the 496 had had their charges dismissed *on the same day* that they were committed "awaiting trial." The curious procedural myopia which led to such travesties can only be speculated about at this point. It is difficult to understand why these courts did not find it incumbent upon them to inform the defendant or the hospitals when charges were dismissed. It is clear from this project and the work of the office of legal counsel of the Department of Mental Health that the courts have rarely notified the "defendant" or his host institution. What a waste of human lives and liberty all this imports.

E. The *Jackson* v. *Indiana* Decision of the U.S. Supreme Court (1972)

On June 7, 1972, the United States Supreme Court handed down *Jackson* v. *Indiana* (No. 70-5009), in which the court cited and adopted the logic of the *Druken* decision. In this unanimous decision (Mr. Justice Blackmun delivered the opinion), the Court established that both the due process and equal protection clauses of the Constitution required that a defendant, who is found to be incompetent to stand trial must also receive the procedural civil requirements. The decision also established that the defendant must meet the standards required for involuntary civil commitment in a given State before he can be subjected to prolonged commitment and must be released when he no longer meets civil commitment standards. In taking this position the Court cited among other "empirical data" one of these papers produced by this project (McGarry 1969).

The *Jackson* decision also addressed itself to the question of the length of time a committed incompetent could be held without prosecution, citing the Sixth and Fourteenth Amendments to the Constitution (the right to a speedy trial and due process clauses). Although the Court did not take a clear position on this issue, it opened the door for the Indiana courts who "should have the first opportunity to determine the issues."

Finally, in *Jackson* the Court (citing, among others, Massachusetts' new Act at *Massachusetts General Laws*, Chapter 123, Section 17, again largely a product of this project) addressed itself to the issue of whether there should be provisions "permitting pretrial motions or even allowing the incompetent defendant a trial at which to establish his innocence without permitting a conviction." The Court commented that its previous decisions did not "preclude the States from allowing, at a minimum, an incompetent defendant to raise certain defenses . . . through counsel" and again opened the door for the Indiana court to review these "possibilities" on further review of the *Jackson* case.

F. Rule 74 of the Massachusetts District Court

During the spring and summer of 1970, the principal investigator was approached by representatives of the Boston Legal Assistance Project, a federally funded group committed to serving the legal needs of the indigent. Attorneys from this group had become disturbed by what they regarded as abuse of discretion in the ordering of pretrial *observational* commitments by certain of the District Courts of Boston. The attorneys were concerned that the 35-day admission orders were being issued inappropriately and with inadequate consideration of the need for mental hospital (Bridgewater in particular) admissions. This legal brief was based on an application of the principles laid down in *Druken* v. *Commonwealth*. The principal investigator agreed to testify before the Supreme Judicial Court in a test case. However, as with one or two earlier cases, the issue was moot by the fact that the patient-defendant had already been discharged from the hospital by the time his case was reached on the High Court's calendar.

At this point Deputy Assistant Attorney General Harold Brown (who had represented the Commonwealth in the cases referred to) acted on a suggestion by Associate Justice Spiegel of the Supreme Judicial Court that the rule-making authority of the Court was a more appropriate and effective avenue to correct or prevent the alleged abuses. Mr. Brown consulted with the principal investigator and proceeded to prepare a legal memorandum with a suggested rule and new official form designed for the ordering of these pretrial admissions. In his memo, which was submitted to Chief Justice Nash of the District Courts (misdemeanor) and ultimately reached the Judicial Council of the Supreme Judicial Court, Mr. Brown quoted extensively from published papers of this project. His brief proved to be persuasive and Rule 74 was promulgated on August 7, 1970. In effect this becomes administrative law for the courts of Massachusetts and binds the judges to follow its requirements.

So far as the District Misdemeanor Courts are concerned, rule 74 in essence restricts the use of pretrial *observational* commitments to the issue of *competency alone*. In addition, the rule requires the judges to justify such order of commitment with adequate accompanying data and requires that the judge himself "interrogate the defendant and any other persons interested and satisfy himself that commitment is necessary. Such determination shall be accom-

57

panied by a finding in writing of the reasons and considerations therefore." It is too early to assess the impact this rule will have on the handling of the competency issue. Certainly it makes explicit the only grounds for such an observational commitment and puts the judge on notice that he must justify and defend such order of commitment.

G. The Group for the Advancement of Psychiatry

In November 1970, the principal investigator became a member of the Committee on Psychiatry and the Law of the Group for the Advancement of Psychiatry. Over the 6 months prior to his election, this committee had been considering the timeliness and need for a GAP report on competency to stand trial. The Committee is now committed to producing such a document. The findings and recommendations of this project will be part of the input of the GAP report. It is premature to speculate about the form and substance the report will ultimately take, nor is it a certainty that it will be published. It does offer the prospect of wide and prestigious dissemination of the project's findings and products.

H. *Nason* v. *Superintendant of Bridgewater State Hospital,* 1968[5]

Early in the work of the grant, an action was brought by the Massachusetts Defenders Committee on the issue of the "right to treatment" of a man committed to Bridgewater as incompetent while awaiting trial for an alleged first degree murder. The principal investigator testified on the issue before the Commissioner appointed by the Supreme Judicial Court of Massachusetts. Most of the testimony given related to the work which was a precursor to this project. The Supreme Judicial Court in its findings on the *Nason* case, citing the work of the Boston University Law-Medicine Institute as a commendable exception, found the treatment offered to committed incompetents at Bridgewater to be inadequate. The court ordered that staff-patient ratios be improved and asserted that the State was required to provide adequate treatment for such patient-defendants. Nason was remanded to the Superior Court and kept at Bridgewater subject to recall and a new review of the case if Nason was not subsequently adequately treated.

---

5. Nason v. Superintendent of Bridgewater State Hospital, 353 Mass. 604, 233 N.E. 2nd 908 (1968).

I. Petition of Rohrer[6]

In a paper published by McGarry (1965), the principal investigator first pointed out serious due process questions in what we have described elsewhere as "mail order commitments." The practices referred to were the indefinite commitment orders emanating from courts on the basis of written reports following observational pretrial admissions. The due process defects in these practices were a lack of notice to the defendant and a lack of opportunity for a judicial hearing to contest such an order. These defects were later documented in a study conducted by the co-principal investigator and principal investigator under the auspices of the Special Commission on Mental Health of the Massachusetts Legislature. It was found that although most Superior Courts of the Commonwealth (felony jurisdiction) did provide a hearing with the defendant present, it was rare for the lower District Courts (misdemeanor jurisdiction), from which the great majority of these commitments emanate, to provide such a hearing. The *Rohrer* case subsequently came down correcting the due process defects cited, although the decision did not necessarily have any direct connection with the published work of the project staff.

The *Rohrer* decision has made a difference in that a few men at Bridgewater have had their criminal status dissolved. Most of the men who were commited as incompetent are now getting a hearing. But as is described elsewhere, these hearings, particularly in the District Courts, tend to be brief and *pro forma* (Rosenberg 1970a).

J. Mental Health Program Reports

Through the offices of Julius Segal, Ph.D., Chief of Program and Analysis Branch of the National Institute of Mental Health and the assistance of his representative, Mrs. Ralph Wittenberg, the principal investigator collaborated in the fall of 1970 in the preparation of a description of the work of this project. This description became part of the fifth volume of *Mental Health Program Reports* and has been widely disseminated.

K. Citation by the First Federal Circuit Court of Appeals

In a recent case,[7] Chief Justice Bailey Aldrich of the First Circuit Court of Appeals cited a paper produced in this project by a

---

6. Petition of Rohrer, 353 Mass. 282, 230 N.E. 2nd 915 (1967).

7. Petition of Harman, Misc. No. 377, United States Court of Appeals for the First Circuit, May 6, 1970.

research attorney (Rosenberg 1970b). The thrust of Justice Aldrich's opinion in the cited case was that Federal defendants committed as incompetent to stand trial should have vigilant judicial followup of their status in order that they not languish for long periods awaiting trial.

L. The Baxstrom-Rohrer Judicial Reviews at Bridgewater

Although the work of this project had a very minor role in the large scale judicial hearings at Bridgewater in 1967, 1968, and 1969, the outcome of these reviews has had such a substantial impact at Bridgewater, that they are worthy of description here.

The *Baxstrom* v. *Herold*[8] decision of the United States Supreme Court in 1966 was interpreted by the then Massachusetts Attorney General Elliott Richardson as requiring the *retroactive* judicial review of the constitutionality of the commitment of many of Birdgewater's patients. A similar interpretation in New York had led to extraordinary changes at Dannemora and Matteawan in New York (Hunt, Wiley 1967). In essence, the *Baxstrom* decision required that men committed to specialized security mental hospitals such as Bridgewater, who were not actually serving criminal sentences, were entitled to the same due process safeguards as patients committed elsewhere in mental hospitals. In addition, the committing court is required by the *Baxstrom* decision to make a separate finding that "strict security is required" before commitment to a security institution is justified and constitutional. The impact of this decision led to a review of patients who had accumulated at Bridgewater over the years whose criminal sentences had expired. The reviewing justice also interpreted the decision as covering men committed to Bridgewater as incompetent to stand trial who had served enough time there, so that if they had been convicted of their alleged crime they would already have reached parole eligiblity (a principle which had been articulated in the early drafts of the Mental Health Reform Act of 1970).

Representatives of the Attorney General's office consulted with the project staff in preparing and drafting the legislation (Chapter 620 and Chapter 621, *Acts of 1967*) which implemented the Attorney General's opinion and set up the large scale judicial reviews.

In all, 267 men were reviewed in June and October of 1968. The principal investigator, representing the Department of Mental Health, organized and supervised screening psychiatric examinations of all these men. He also supervised testimony in those cases in

---

8. Baxstrom v. Herold, 383 U.S. 107 (1966).

which the Department of Mental Health felt there was sufficient danger to others should they be released from Bridgewater. Only 22 out of the 267 men were evaluated as dangerous. Only 9 of the 22 were recommitted to Bridgewater by the Presiding Justice. Most of these men were transferred to Department of Mental Health facilities (N=240). In an unpublished followup study by the principal investigator (N=234), 43 percent of these men had reached the community by June of 1971.

These significant reductions at Bridgewater change a census which had approached 800 in the early 1960's to 245 in December 1970. These changes were brought about by the significantly fewer men being indefinitely committed in the past few years (particularly the incompetent for trial group), recent policy changes in the Department of Mental Health which have opened its institutions to Bridgewater transfers, and new activism on the part of the Bridgewater staff in negotiating with courts to resolve criminal charges. Of these 245, only 158 were indefinite commitments. Eighty-seven were observational commitments. These statistics are all the more impressive when one notes that over the decade Bridgewater pretrial observational admissions sharply rose (from 129 in 1960 to 501 in 1971).

More important to note is that Bridgewater has clearly been transformed from a custodial to an actively treatment-oriented facility. Professional staff has been impressively augmented (from 3 phsyicians in 1963 to 7 in 1970; from 1 nurse in 1963 to 30; from 4 social workers to 7), and links to the community, such as tutors and student volunteers from Bridgewater State Teachers College, have been developed. There is a new spirit of activism at the institution. What is sometimes lacking in sophistication in these programs is made up for in zeal. Ground breaking for a new, cottage type $10,000,000 institution at Bridgewater took place in 1971. Although it does not yet approach a model institution for mentally disordered offenders there is no question that much has been accomplished over the last few years.

61

Commentary on Significant Issues Related to Competency Proceedings And Recommendations for Reform

A. The Significance and Scope of the Project

This project has taken place in the Commonwealth of Massachusetts. As such, it has its greatest relevance to the practices in this State. Compared to the rest of the country, Massachusetts appears to be somewhat atypical in the large numbers of judicial orders for pretrial psychiatric examinations on the issues of competency and criminal responsibility. Part of this is a tradition which goes back to the often cited "Briggs Law" which was passed in 1921 (formerly *Massachusetts General Laws*, Chapter 123, Section 100A). This statute provided for the automatic pretrial psychiatric examination of all capital cases and repeating felons on the issue of criminal responsibility. What is not widely known is that the operation of this statute has been a failure. Less than one thousand out of possibly ten thousand such required examinations a year actually took place. The reasons for this failure are at least two-fold. The first is that Massachusetts does not have the psychiatric manpower to implement the statute, and the second is the low fee provided for these examinations. The fee for such an examination and report was $7.00. The "Briggs Law" has now been repealed by Chapter 888, *Massachusetts Acts of 1970*, which took effect on November 1, 1971.

The failure of the "Briggs Law" may be part of the reason why pretrial admissions to our mental hospitals were resorted to in such large numbers. Other purposes are being served by these admissions, some of them laudable at first glance. They include the seeking of dispositional alternatives to prison, preventive detention, strategic and other considerations. Until recently in this State, these procedures were a more easily invoked alternative to the procedurally onerous civil commitment procedures and they provided for our courts a *mandated* admission to our mental hospitals, whereas civil procedures leave admission to the discretion of the admitting physicians of our hospitals.

In contrast to Massachusetts, MacDonald, after extensive forensic experience in Colorado, could remember only one occasion when the issue of competency was raised (MacDonald 1969). However, in the context of the increasing challege, distrust, and hostility abroad in the country regarding involuntary civil commitment of the mentally ill (despite the achievements of the past decade in improving the treatment of the mentally ill), we would predict the increasing use of criminal procedures under the competency rubric. But, as we have learned in Massachusetts, the status of alleged criminality, when added to that of mental illness, has invariably led to legal and therapeutic neglect of such individuals. To be both "mad" and "bad" is to be doubly damned, and excessive conservatism regarding release into the community of such individuals has been the rule.

Those who do not learn from Massachusetts' reforms in this area may be destined to repeat her history. Perhaps the results of this study, adequately disseminated, will serve in other jurisdictions to prevent the misuse of competency procedures as we have described them.

B. Are Psychiatrists the Only Experts on Competency?

In an older Massachusetts case,[1] Mr. Chief Justice Rugg wrote:

> The judge who denied the motion presided over the jury trial, saw the defendant, heard him testify in his own behalf, and of course watched his apparent mental capacity as revealed both under direct and cross-examination and by his other conduct in the courtroom during the trial. The judge may well have been able to form a judgment as to legal responsibility of the defendant for crime, based upon common sense inferences and intelligent observation, more reliable as a practical guide to accomplishment of justice than the refined distinctions and technical niceties of alienists and experts in psychopathic inferiority.

Although Chief Justice Rugg confuses and intermingles "present sanity" with "sanity at the time of the crime," there is merit in his statements. Ideally, the judge should question the defendant and perhaps his attorney as well before he reached a decision on competency. But it is clear that, in large measure, in our heavily burdened courts, the judges we have observed have abdicated their authority and delegated ultimate decision-making on the issue to psychiatrists. As we have seen, until recent years in Massachusetts,

---

1. Commonwealth v. Devereaux, 257 Mass. 391, 153 N.E. 881 (1926).

psychiatrists have poorly understood this legal issue and out of ignorance have participated, albeit reluctantly and with good intent, in these procedures, to the detriment of their patients.

There appear to be four basic requirements for an examiner or "expert" on the issue of competency: (1) an adequate knowledge of the criminal justice system; (2) adequate interpersonal skills in interviewing and eliciting relevant, legally-oriented data from defendants who are mentally ill or mentally retarded; (3) knowledge and application of criteria for competency; and (4) professional status to assure credibility. Given these requirements it is at once apparent that psychiatrists (and psychologists and social workers), unless they have had adequate criminal process experience, are likely to lack sufficient knowledge of the criminal justice system and knowledge and application of criteria for competency. Lawyers (with criminal bar experience) will be strong in the first but generally weak in the second. We would suggest that any of the three alternative professional groups mentioned (as well as others), with adequate training and experience in their weaker area, could do at least as satisfactory a job in competency proceedings as psychiatrists have up to now. The three research attorneys who have worked on this project and who have become familiar and comfortable with the interviewing of mentally ill persons, very quickly attained as much expertise regarding competency as the research psychiatrists, all of whom have had extensive forensic experience with the competency issue.

As has been noted, an attempt has been made through legislation to establish a system of legal advisors (attorneys) in Massachusetts mental hospitals. These advisors would have had independent authority to periodically review the competency of committed incompetents and would have had authority to invoke a competency hearing regardless of the opinions of the psychiatrists in charge of the patient. The procedural model elected was that the legal advisor would not be a party to the proceedings other than as an expert witness. If he were in the traditional adversary role, he would have a conflict in his loyalty and responsibilities. Mental health professionals who have clinical responsibilities for treating these patient-defendants, unfortunately are often placed in the conflicting position of having to testify against the wishes of their patients.

Tradition and precedent die particularly hard in legal practice and it is likely that psychiatrists will continue to be ordered to produce "expert" opinions on the competency issue. It follows that such expertise should be real and not assumed, and special forensic training or experience is required to responsibly answer such orders. Whatever innovative alternatives are developed, the psychiatrist will appropriately continue to carry primary *treatment* responsibility for the incompetent.

C. Base Rates of Incompetency

Demographic data from 2 years of pretrial observational patients at Bridgewater are recorded elsewhere in this report (see Chapter III). It will therefore be possible for other jurisdictions to compare their populations and their rates of incompetency findings to those in Massachusetts. In 1971, Bridgewater found only 6 out of 501 observational admissions to be incompetent. It is our impression that this is an accurate frequency based on our experience at Bridgewater and in the courts of the Commonwealth over the past 6 years. It follows that valid incompetency for trial is a rather rare phenomenon. It is also a transitory phenomenon in that the great majority of acute psychotics are responsive to current treatment modalities and can be expected to regain a competent state within weeks to months of active treatment. The very rare severe mental retardate who gets caught in the competency net may be an exception to this generalization.

D. Necessary and Recommended Reforms

In the light of the work of this project and the documentation of abuses and inequities contained in this report and in the publications of others in the field, consideration of the following procedural and substantive principles in competency proceedings are recommended.

1. *Only when a bona fide doubt is established regarding an accused's competency for trial should competency proceedings be invoked.*

2. *A screening examination by a qualified expert (not necessarily a psychiatrist) should be carried out in the courthouse or place of detention or on an outpatient basis.* The examiner should be provided with the police arrest report and such other data as are available with relation to the facts of the case.

3. *If, after such screening examination, a doubt still exists, more intensive and prolonged examination should take place.* Consideration should be given to accomplishing such examination on an outpatient basis. If necessary, brief, observational inpatient hospitalization may be ordered and such order of admission should be accompanied by the police arrest report

and such other data as are available with relation to the facts of the case. The period of observational admission should have no minimum term.

4. *Appropriate notice of and a prompt judicial hearing on the competency issue should be given to the patient-defendant with independent expert examination available to the defense.*

5. *A presumption of competency should exist which is rebuttable only if, by a "preponderance of evidence," the accused is found, after an adequate judicial hearing, to be incompetent to stand trial.*

6. *Procedures should be available whereby an incompetent defendant and/or his counsel may present evidence of a defense on the merits without risk of conviction.* The granting of a judicial hearing to consider such evidence should be up to the discretion of the trial judge following an affidavit requesting such a hearing from the defense counsel or the defendant. The basis for such request should be expressed in such an affidavit. The prosecution should be represented at the hearing. Following the hearing, if the trial judge finds a lack of substantial evidence to support a conviction, he should dismiss the indictment or other charges and order the release of the defendant from criminal custody, or he should reduce the charges to those for which substantial evidence to support a conviction does exist.

7. *Following a finding of incompetence, full civil safeguards and procedures now must be provided if prolonged mental hospital commitment is sought (cf. Jackson v. Indiana in Chapter VI).* Consideration should be given to outpatient or partial hospitalization of the patient-defendant.

8. *A "statute of limitations" should be running at the time of a finding of incompetency.* Various formulae could be adopted depending on social policy in a given jurisdiction, but no defendant should be kept in criminal custody with charges still outstanding for longer than he could have been sentenced if he was found guilty of the most serious crime with which he is charged. Further hospitalization beyond such term should be on a voluntary or civil basis with charges dismissed.

9. *Flexible management of committed incompetents, including outpatient management, by the administrators of the holding institution should be possible.* Notice to the committing court of proposed decreased controls over the patient-defendant could be given to the prosecutor and the commit-

ting court. But only after a judicial hearing, called within a limited period of time, should such a decrease in controls be subject to a countermanding order by the committing court.

10. *Periodic clinical review of committed incompetents should be required every 3 months of such commitment and easily invoked periodic judicial review at the same interval by any of the parties (i.e., defendant, defense counsel, prosecution) should be available.* The judge or hospital administrator should be able to invoke a prompt judicial review of the competency issue at any time.

E. The Problems Behind the Problem

It is of great significance that, although the psychiatrists of the mental health system in Massachusetts appear to be doing a better job by indefinitely committing very few of the defendants being sent to them, the courts (prior to the Mental Health Reform Act of 1971) continued to send defendants in every-increasing numbers. These hospitalizations under the competency rubric were increasingly inappropriate and unnecessary. Throughout Massachusetts, for example, in fiscal 1970, only 6 percent of 2,101 observational admissions were found to be incompetent. Therefore, the courts were casting a wider and wider net to catch fewer and fewer men and doing a good deal of harm in the stigmatization of increasing numbers of defendants, a majority of whom were alleged misdemeanants, in an increasingly unnecessary procedure. As is noted in Chapter VI, these abuses have been substantially reduced under the Mental Health Reform Act.

If followed that a major task confronted us to educate (or require) the courts to use screening procedures (such as the use of the Competency Screening Test and screening psychiatric examinations) so that wasteful and potentially damaging admissions to our overtaxed hospitals could be cut down. As has been noted in significant measure, these purposes have been accomplished in Massachusetts.

These courts are obviously seeking something from our hospitals other than competency determinations *per se*. It appears that our desperately overtaxed courts are seeking constructive alternatives to the criminal justice and penal systems as they currently exist. If the competency route has been a false solution and has accomplished more harm than good, we must seek ways in which the courts and their disturbed offenders can be more effectively helped by the behavioral disciplines. Possibly, our emerging community mental

67

health centers, utilizing civil and voluntary procedures for alleged offenders, may yet make a significant contribution.

Our mental health resources must be more creatively and effectively deployed in attempting to meet these great challenges. We must more constructively integrate and advance the social and rehabilitative aims that are common to both the mental health and criminal justice systems.

References

Armor, D.J., and Couch, A.S. *The Data-Text Primer: An Introduction to Computerized Social Data Analysis Using the Data-Text System.* New York: Free Press, forthcoming.

Balcanoff, E.J., and McGarry, A.L. Amicus curiae: The role of the psychiatrist in pre-trial examination. *American Journal of Psychiatry,* 126:342-347, 1969.

Brozek, J., and Schiele, B.C. Clinical significance of the Minnesota Multiphasic F Scale evaluated in experimental neurosis. *American Journal of Psychiatry,* 105:259-266, 1948.

Bukataman, B.A.; Foy, J.L.; and DeGrazia, E. What is competency to stand trial? *American Journal of Psychiatry,* 127:1225-1229, 1971.

Fiske, D.W., and Van Buskirk, C. The Stability of interpretation of sentence completion tests. *Journal of Consulting Psychology,* 23:170-180, 1959.

Goldberg, P.A. A review of sentence completion methods in personality assessment. *Journal of Projective Techniques,* 29:12-45, 1965.

Haggard, E.A. *Intraclass Correlation and the Analysis of Variance.* New York: Dryden Press, 1968.

Harman, H.H. *Modern Factor Analysis.* Chicago: University of Chicago Press, 1964.

Hess, J.H., and Thomas, T.E. Incompetency to stand trial: Procedures, results and problems. *American Journal of Psychiatry,* 119:713-720, 1963.

Hunt, R.C., and Wiley, E.D. "Operation Baxstrom after One Year." A paper read at the Annual Meeting of the American Psychiatric Association, Detroit, Michigan, May, 1967.

Judicial Conference of the District of Columbia Circuit. *Report of the Committee on Problems Connected with Mental Examinations of the Accused in Criminal Cases Before Trial.* Washington, D.C.: Institute of Criminal Law and Procedure, Georgetown University Law Center, 1966.

Karen, R.L. A method for rating sentence completion test responses. *Journal of Projective Techniques,* 25:312-314, 1961.

Lyerly, S.B., and Abbott, T.S. *Handbook of Psychiatric Rating Scales.* (PHS Publication No. 1495) Washington, D.C.: Superintendent of Documents, U.S. Government Printing Office, 1965.

Lipsitt, P.D.; Lelos, D.; and McGarry, A.L. Competency for trial: A screening instrument. *American Journal of Psychiatry,* 128:105-109, 1971.

MacDonald, J.M. *Psychiatry and the Criminal.* Springfield, Ill.: Charles C Thomas, 1969, second edition.

Matthews, A.R. *Mental Illness and the Criminal Law: Is Community Mental Health an Answer?* Chicago: American Bar Foundation, 1966.

Matthews, A.R. *Mental Disability and the Criminal Law.* Chicago: American Bar Foundation, 1970.

McGarry, A.L. Competency for trial and due process via the State hospital. *American Journal of Psychiatry*, 122:623-630, 1965.

McGarry, A.L., and Bendt, R.H. Civil vs. criminal commitment of psychotic offenders: A seven year follow-up. *American Journal of Psychiatry*, 125:1387-1394, 1969.

McGarry, A.L. The fate of psychotic offenders returned for trial. *American Journal of Psychiatry*, 127:1181-1184, 1971.

McGarry, A.L., and Schwitzgebel, R.K. "Inter-rater Reliability and a New Instrument." Paper read at the American Psychiatric Association meeting, 1972, in Dallas, Texas.

Morris, N. Impediments to legal reform. *University of Chicago Law Review*, 33:627-656, 1966.

Rao, C.R. *Advanced Statistical Methods in Biomedical Research.* New York: Wiley and Sons, 1962.

Robey, A. Criteria for competency to stand trial: A checklist for psychiatrists. *American Journal of Psychiatry*, 122:616-622, 1965.

Rosenberg, A.H. "Competency for Trial: Observations of Court Practices in Massachusetts Courts." (unpublished paper, 1970a).

Rosenberg, A.H. Competency for trial: A problem in interdisciplinary communication. *Judicature*, 53:314-321, 1970b.

Rosenberg, A.H., and McGarry, A.L. Competency for trial: The making of an expert. *American Journal of Psychiatry*, 128:1092-1096, 1972.

Rotter, J.B., and Willerman, B. The Incomplete Sentence Test as a method of studying personality. *Journal of Consulting Psychology*, 11:43-48, 1947.

Scheidemandel, P.L., and Kanno, C.K. *The Mentally Ill Offender: A Survey of Treatment Programs.* Washington, D.C.: Joint Information Service, 1969.

Schwitzgebel, R.K. Ethical problems in experimentation with offenders. *American Journal of Orthopsychiatry*, 38:738-748, 1968.

Settle, R.D. and Oppergard, C.R. Institute of Sentencing Appendix C. The Pre-trial Examination of Federal Defendants. 35 F.R.D. 381:475-482, 1964.

APPENDIX A

COMPETENCY SCREENING TEST

Contents

THE NATURE OF COMPETENCY

To be fit for trial, it is assumed that person must have minimal affective and cognitive resources available to him to assume the role of a defendant in court. Lacking these resources, the individual would be deprived of his due process right to testify in his own defense, to confront witnesses against him, and to maintain an effective *psychological presence* in court beyond his mere physical presence there. The issue of competency is thus an essentially legal issue, not a psychiatric issue. The criteria for competency to stand trial are concerned with the protection of the individual in the criminal system in order that he may be assured of a fair trial. No other area of the person's physical or emotional health is an issue. Whether or not the person has physical or psychological defects is irrelevant except to the extent that they substantially interfere with fitness for trial.

The common law criteria for competency are defined as (1) an ability to cooperate with one's attorney in one's own defense, (2) an awareness and understanding of the nature and object of the proceedings, (3) an understanding of the consequences of the proceedings. Within the framework of these criteria, a judgment must be made as to whether an accused person should stand trial without undue delay or whether the trial should be deferred until such time as the accused shall meet a minimal standard based on these criteria.

The determination of competency in the broadest sense must be based on some evaluation of these criteria. It must be a prediction because the judgment of the actual performance of the defendant in the role of defendant has not occurred. An assessment of the defendant's ability to perform adequately at his trial must be made by individuals considered most expert to evaluate fitness for trial.

It is important that the assessment or evaluation of the defendant be made with a clear understanding of the requirements of the legal system. Psychological evaluation must be directed toward determining how well the individual will be able to meet the minimum requirements of the three common law criteria for competency. Issues such as legal responsibility for the offense or possibility of rehabilitation are not relevant considerations. Also, mental illness or pathology *per se* are not equivalent to capacity to stand trial, although such matters may be involved in a determination of competency.

The test which follows has been developed for the purpose of quickly screening defendants in order to make recommendations regarding their competency to stand trial. This test is an experimental instrument, and the evaluation of its validity and reliability is continuing.

ADMINISTRATION OF THE COMPETENCY SCREENING TEST

This paper and pencil test is based on 22 sentence completion stems that are administered to the subject with the following instructions:

Here are some incomplete sentences dealing with court-room situations. Each one has something to do with the law and going to court. There are no right or wrong answers. Your first impressions is usually the best. If, for any reason, you cannot complete a sentence, please circle the number and go on to the next one.

Each item can be scored, 0, 1, or 2; higher scores indicate high levels on the competency scale. To arrive at a total score of competency for each individual, item scores are summed. A total score below 20 has been judged in early analysis to raise the issue of competency.

THE COMPETENCY SCREENING TEST*

1. The lawyer told Bill that

2. When I go to court the lawyer will

3. Jack felt that the judge

4. When Phil was accused of the crime, he

5. When I prepare to go to court with my lawyer

6. If the jury finds me guilty, I

7. The way a court trial is decided

8. When the evidence in George's case was presented to the jury

9. When the lawyer questioned his client in court, the client said

10. If Jack has to try his own case, he

11. Each time the D.A. asked me a question, I

12. While listening to the witnesses testify against me, I

13. When the witness testifying against Harry gave incorrect evidence, he

14. When Bob disagreed with his lawyer on his defense, he

15. When I was formally accused of the crime, I though to myself

16. If Ed's lawyer suggests that he plead guilty, he

17. What concerns Fred most about his lawyer

18. When they say a man is innocent until proven guilty

19. When I think of being sent to prison, I

20. When Phil thinks of what he is accused of, he

21. When the jury hears my case, they will

22. If I had a chance to speak to the judge, I

HANDBOOK FOR SCORING THE TEST*

1. The lawyer told Bill that

    (a) Legal criteria: ability to cooperate in own defense, communicate, relate
    (b) Psychological criteria: ability to relate or trust

    SCORE 2: includes obtaining and/or accepting advice or guidance

    examples: "he should plead not guilty"
    "he was free"
    "he should plead nolo"
    "he should plead guilty"
    "he would take his case"
    "he would need to know all the facts concerning the case"
    "he should turn himself in"
    "the outlook was good"
    "he will try to help him"

    SCORE 1:

    examples: "he is innocent"
    "everything is all right"
    "be truthful"
    "he will be going to court soon"
    "he is competent to stand trial"
    "it will be filed"

    SCORE 0: includes regarding lawyer as accusing or judgmental

    examples: "he was wrong in doing what he did"
    "he is guilty"
    "he is going to be put away"
    "no comment"

2. When I go to court the lawyer will

    (a) Legal criteria: ability to cooperate in own defense, communicate, relate.
    (b) Psychological criteria: ability to relate or trust

    SCORE 2:

    examples: "defend me"

*Copyright © Paul D. Lipsitt and David Lelos, 1970. Used by permission.

"be there to help me"
"do his best to get me off with a light sentence"
"represent me"
"present my case"

SCORE 1:
examples: "be there"
"ask for postponement"
"ask me to take the stand"

SCORE 0:
examples: "put me away"
"keep his mouth shut"
"prosecute me"

3. Jack felt that the judge

(a) Legal criteria: understanding and awareness of court process
(b) Psychological criteria: awareness and acceptance of court process

SCORE 2:
examples: "was right"
"was fair"
"tried to keep an open mind"
"was a rough judge to face on his particular charge"

SCORE 1:
examples: "was doing his job"

SCORE 0:
examples: "was unjust"
"was wrong"
"was too harsh"
"was his enemy"
"no comment"

4. When Phil was accused of the crime, he

(a) Legal criteria: understanding and awareness of the consequences
(b) Psychological criteria: appropriate coping attitude/emotion

SCORE 2: includes appropriate response to a formal accusation as in a courtroom situation
examples: "pleaded not quilty"
"got a lawyer"

77

SCORE 1: includes appropriate emotion without coping as a positive outcome not appropriate to the stem

examples: "could,not believe it"
"shivered"
"felt nervous"
"was arrested"
"was innocent"
"denied it"
"was let free"

SCORE 0:

examples: "pleaded guilty"
"confessed"
"wanted what was coming to him"
"wasn't himself"

5. When I prepare to go to court with my lawyer

   (a) Legal criteria: ability to cooperate in own defense, communicate, relate
   (b) Psychological criteria: appropriate coping attitude/emotion

   SCORE 2:

   examples: "we will know that we are ready"
   "I will tell him the truth"
   "I hope to win"
   "we will have long talks"

   SCORE 1:

   examples: "everything is all right"
   "he'll tell me to take the stand"
   "he does the talking for me"
   "I felt better"
   "I feel nervous"

   SCORE 0:

   examples: "I will go to court with my lawyer and my family"
   "they tried me"
   "he will change his mind and set me free"
   "I will get a fine"

6. If the jury find me guilty, I

   (a) Legal criteria: understanding and awareness of consequences
   (b) Psychological criteria: realistic assessment of consequences

   SCORE 2:

   examples: "will go to jail"

"will serve my sentence"
"will appeal"
"will ask my lawyer what to do"
"will pay a fine"

SCORE 1: includes passive acceptance of fate

examples: "will have to take whatever sentence I get"
"will be mad"
"take the punishment"
"go where they send me"
"will do life"
"accept the decision"
"will try to be calm"
"will feel very bad"

SCORE 0:

examples: "the only thing I can say is I'm *Not* guilty"
"will be back"
"I think I'll hate the world"
"will die"
"will be sentenced to the maximum penalty"

7. The way a court trial is decided

   (a) Legal criteria: understanding and awareness of court process
   (b) Psychological criteria: ability to select correct information

   SCORE 2:

   examples: "is by the evidence"
   "is by the jury"
   "is by the judge and jury"
   "is the judge decides"
   "is based on the facts given"

   SCORE 1: also includes awareness of the role of the lawyer

   examples: "is fair"
   "is up to the laws of the state"
   "by the court"
   "is through due process of the law"
   "depends on the way your lawyer presents the case"

   SCORE 0:

   examples: "is whether he is able to stand to trial"
   "is open for improvement"
   "is always by a lawyer"
   "is on the majority of opinion"
   "is for the people"

79

"guilty — not guilty"

8. When the evident in George's case was presented to the jury

    (a) Legal criteria: understanding and awareness of consequences
    (b) Psychological criteria: appropriate emotion and/or coping

        SCORE 2: includes awareness of jury's function and procedures

           examples: "they listened carefully to the evidence presented to them"
                      "felt his lawyer had done his job"
                      "the case was dismissed"
                      "they found him not guilty"
                      "they were fair in judgement"
                      "he was very worried"
                      "they deliberated and reached a verdict"

        SCORE 1:

           examples: "they retired"
                      "he remained calm"
                      "the case was settled right away"

        SCORE 0: includes expectation of losing

           examples: "he was found guilty"
                      "he felt persecuted"
                      "they looked bewildered"
                      "it was presented wrong"
                      "he cried"

9. When the lawyer question his client in court, the client said

    (a) Legal criteria: ability to cooperate in own defense, communicate, relate
    (b) Psychological criteria: appropriate coping attitude

        SCORE 2:

           examples: "the answer to whatever question was asked"
                      "I am not guilty"
                      "I did not do anything"

        SCORE 1: includes overspecificity, vagueness and/or hesitancy to cooperate with lawyer

           examples: "he did not know the person in question"
                      "he had no knowledge of it"
                      "I don't know why — not quilty"

        SCORE 0:

           examples: "the obvious things"

"he's guilty"

"I refuse to answer on the grounds that I may incriminate myself"

"he was too nervous to talk"

10. If Jack had to try his own case, he

(a) Legal criteria: understanding and awareness of the court process

(b) Psychological criteria: acknowledgment of need for attorney and recognition of complexity of situation

SCORE 2:

examples: "would not know where to begin"

"would lose"

"would refuse"

"would try to make the jury understand"

SCORE 1:

examples: "would tell the truth"

"could offer substantial defense"

"would plead not guilty"

"would proceed with it"

SCORE 0:

examples: "would possibly make a good lawyer"

"would set himself free"

"would plead guilty"

11. Each time the D.A. asked me a question, I

(a) Legal criteria: understanding and awareness of court process

(b) Psychological criteria: responses that reflect appropriate behavior of defendant

SCORE 2:

examples: "thought before I answered him"

"told the truth"

"answered"

"refused to answer because my lawyer was not present"

"would listen very carefully"

SCORE 1:

examples: "get nervous"

"would take a long time"

SCORE 0:

examples: "stood mute"

81

"would say I don't know"
"take the fifth"
"not guilty"

12. While listening to the witnesses testify against me, I

   (a) Legal criteria; understanding and awareness of court process
   (b) Psychological criteria: ability to adequately attend to the sequence of court events and his relationship to it

   SCORE 2:

   examples: "would listen carefully"
   "listened to find out if they were presenting any perjury"
   "began to remember pertinent details"

   SCORE 1: includes appropriate contentiousness

   examples: "listened"
   "was getting very mad"
   "prayed"
   "got nervous"
   "felt they were lying"

   SCORE 0: includes inappropriate court room behavior

   examples: "laughed"
   "got bored"
   "agreed"
   "denied their testimony"

13. When the witness testifying against Harry gave incorrect evidence, he

   (a) Legal criteria: understanding and awareness of court process
   (b) Psychological criteria: ability to adequately attend to the sequence of court events and his relationship to it

   SCORE 2:

   examples: "was perjuring himself"
   "informed his lawyer"
   "asked for a conference with his lawyer"
   "objected to it"

   SCORE 1:

   examples: "lied"
   "got mad"
   "was hurt"
   "was wrong"

82

"was not guilty"

SCORE 0:

examples: "stood up and said it was a lie"
"laughed"
"thought he could not do anything"

14. When Bob disagreed with his lawyer on his defense, he

(a) Legal criteria: ability to cooperate in hiw own defense and communicate with his lawyer
(b) Psychological criteria: ability to trust and appropriately express self-protective attitude

SCORE 2: must include attempt to reconcile or compromise

examples: "argued his point"
"asked for a ten minute recess"
"deferred to his lawyer"

SCORE 1: includes appropriate uncommunicated emotion, evaluative comment or statement of outcome

examples: "was right"
"was wrong"
"was mad"
"complicated matters"
"was advised to do as he was told"

SCORE 0: characterized by withdrawal or refusal to cooperate

examples: "got another lawyer"
"figured there was no sense arguing"

15. When I was formally accused of the crime, I thought to myself

(a) Legal criteria: awareness of the peril of his situation
(b) Psychological criteria: an appreciation of personal involvement in the legal system

SCORE 2:

examples: "how wrong"
"I did not do it"
"what if they found me guilty"
"I knew I was in trouble"

SCORE 1:

examples: "it wasn't my fault"
"how foolish I've been"
"the law could use some modification"

"this can't be happening"
"I've been framed"

SCORE 0:

    examples: "it's all over"
               "here we go again"
               "it's all for the best"
               "I'm going to jail"

16. If Ed's lawyer suggests that he plead guilty, he

  (a) Legal criteria: understanding and awareness of the court process and ability to cooperate with attorney in own defense
  (b) Psychological criteria: ability to trust and appropriately express self-protective attitude

    SCORE 2:

      examples: "will do so"
               "will probably go along with it"
               "tried to talk over the evidence with his lawyer and then decided"
               "would seek further advice"

    SCORE 1: includes explanation of lawyer's intent without personal involvement

      examples: "would try to get him off on a light sentence"
               "he will disagree"
               "he started to worry"
               "was wrong "

    SCORE 0:

      examples: "he won't do it"
               "he be released"
               "will be put away"

17. What concerns Fred most about his lawyer

  (a) Legal criteria: ability to cooperate in own defense and relate to his attorney
  (b) Psychological criteria: ability to interact constructively with attorney

    SCORE 2: characterized by a concern with lawyer's interest and competence in regard to the case

      examples: "how good he is"
               "the fact that he isn't adequately defending him"

"he doesn't know him too well"
"he is trying to help him"
"he thinks that I am guilty"

SCORE 1: includes concern with general adequacy

examples: "insight into the matter"
"money"
"is he qualified"
"his drive"

SCORE 0:

examples: "his integrity"
"tardiness"
"facts"

18. When they say a man is innocent until proven guilty

   (a) Legal criteria: understanding and awareness of court process
   (b) Psychological criteria: a fundamental understanding of the basic legal concept

   SCORE 2: characterized by understanding that the burden of proof lies with the prosecution

   examples: "just that"
   "exactly what it says"
   "until they get proof against him"
   "that he is not guilty until the jury decides"
   "that everyone has the right to a fair trial"

   SCORE 1:

   examples: "not guilty"
   "that he is innocent"
   "he has to be proven beyond a shadow of a doubt"

   SCORE 0:

   examples: "guilty"
   "nothing"
   "guilty until proven innocent"
   "it's for the judge to decide"

19. When I think of being sent to prison, I

   (a) Legal criteria: Understanding and awareness of the consequences
   (b) Psychological criteria: appropriate affect related to threat of disrupted life and separation

85

SCORE 2:

   examples: "get very depressed"
                 "started to worry about my family"
                 "get scared"
                 "think of the time I shall lose"

SCORE 1:

   examples: "go into a deep depression". (The incapacitating nature of the depression differentiates from above.)
                 "cried"
                 "hope it won't be for very long"
                 "don't feel too good"
                 "feel wrongly accused"
                 "feel uneasy"

SCORE 0:

   examples: "feel like dying"
                 "don't worry"
                 "think that is where I belong"

20. When Phil thinks of what he is accused of, he

   (a) Legal criteria: understanding and awareness of peril of position
   (b) Psychological criteria: appropriate affect related to potential threat to self

   SCORE 2:

      examples: "gets upset"
                    "gets nervous and depressed"
                    "gets angry"
                    "worries about the outcome"

   SCORE 1:

      examples: "is ashamed"
                    "is very sorry for himself"
                    "thinks how foolish he was"
                    "just can't believe it"
                    "wonders why it happened this way"

   SCORE 0:

      examples: "cries"
                    "does not worry"
                    "thinks the law should be changed"

21. When the jury hears my case, they will

(a) Legal criteria: understanding and awareness of the court process
(b) Pyschological criteria: appropriate assessment of role and function of jury

SCORE 2:
examples: "try to be fair"
"find me innocent"
"set me free"
"go along with my defense"
"probably understand"
"say not guilty"

SCORE 1:
examples: "be the ones to decide"
"agree"
"think it over"
"say guilty or not guilty"
"find extenuating circumstances"

SCORE 0:
examples: "be confused by the conflicting opinion"
"laugh"
"say guilty"
"convict me"
"send me to jail"
"not think very much of me"

22. If I had a chance to speak to the judge, I

(a) Legal criteria: capacity to communicate in own defense
(b) Psychological criteria: appropriate communication and trust

SCORE 2:
examples: "would tell my story"
"would try to explain things"
"would aks for a break"
"would cop a plea"

SCORE 1:
examples: "would"
"would feel more happy and relaxed"
"would tell him I am being framed"

SCORE 0:
examples: "will die"
"would say nothing"

87

"it wouldn't do any good"
"would tell him to give me the gas chamber"

THE RESEARCH: COMPETENCY TO STAND TRIAL AND MENTAL ILLNESS

This section is included for those who wish information on the methods followed to develop the test, its historical background and its reliability and validity. It is hoped that this information will be helpful to those who plan to undertake similar research.

During the first year of the study, in the first stage of the development of the Competency Screening Test, samples from several populations were administered an early version of this test. This procedure was used to elicit a wide range of responses to the items to determine if there were differences in the responses as a function of the population backgrounds. Thus, the construction of a final instrument could be based on some base-line data for comparative purposes.

Subjects

The groups that were administered this test during the first year included a group of persons civilly committed to a State hospital; a men's church club; college undergraduates in a juvenile delinquency course; non-hospitalized defendants preparing for trial; and patients committed to a State hospital as a result of criminal proceedings who were in various stages of rehabilitation.

The second year sample of fifty-one subjects* was essentially randomly selected from the total population currently committed for 35 days of competency observation at Bridgewater State Hospital, a high security institution for mentally disturbed patients either accused of crimes or adjudicated as offenders. This sample, which was generally representative of the larger Bridgewater population, was entirely male, 53.1 percent single, 77.5 percent unskilled laborers, 12.0 percent black, and had a mean educational level of 10th grade. The most frequent, alleged offenses were homicide, assault, larceny, and misdemeanors.

The third year sample of fifty-three subjects was specifically selected from the larger Bridgewater population on the basis of some indication of psychosis or mental retardation. This third year sample was also entirely male, 58.0 percent single, 28.0 percent unskilled laborers, 32.1 percent black, and had a mean educational level of 10th grade. Approximately 72.6 percent of this third year sample were given a diagnosis of some form of schizophrenia by

---

*The total N of the second and third year samples varies on certain items of analysis because of some missing or incomplete data.

89

TABLE I. Rotated factor loadings

Variable Description	Item No.	1	2	3	4	5	6
The lawyer told Bill that	1	.734*	.133	.262	.149	-.013	-.067
When I go to court the lawyer will	2	.668*	-.005	.192	-.006	-.144	.333
When I prepare to go to court with my lawyer	5	.567*	.440	-.009	.096	.131	.221
When the lawyer questioned his client in court, the client said	9	-.329	.016	.428*	.449*	.070	.461*
When Bob disagreed with his lawyer on his defense, he	14	.561*	.040	.010	.350	.302	-.037
If Ed's lawyer suggests that he plead guilty, he	16	.146	.069	-.055	.802*	.091	.071
What concerns Fred most about his lawyer	17	.077	.071	.092	.106	.810*	.256
If I had a chance to speak to the judge, I	22	.115	.428	.200	-.261	.237	.523*
Jack felt that the judge	3	.207	.060	.632*	.009	-.347	.190
The way a court trial is decided	7	-.046	.564*	.160	.056	.014	.155
If Jack had to try his own case, he	10	.026	.590*	.008	-.025	.412*	-.102
Each time the D.A. asked me a question, I	11	.180	.271	.234	.315	-.038	.299
While listening to the witnesses testifying against me, I	12	.406*	.085	.491*	.313	.187	.092
When the witness testifying against Harry gave incorrect evidence, he	13	.267	.240	.298	.447*	.278	-.184
When they say a man is innocent until proven guilty	18	.168	.397	.177	.513*	-.123	.104
When the jury hears my case, they will	21	.309	.069	.413*	-.061	.131	.319
When Phil was accused of the crime	4	-.060	.221	.728*	-.054	.233	-.034
If the jury finds me guilty, I	6	.343	.038	.569*	.216	-.019	.129
When the evidence in George's case was presented to the jury	8	.171	.593*	.328	.167	-.107	-.010
When I was formally accused of the crime, I thought to myself	15	.158	.025	.080	.037	.187	.694*
When I think of being sent to prison, I	19	.210	.646*	-.109	.235	.063	.231
When Phil thinks of what he is accused of, he	20	-.008	.355	.022	.263	-.170	.576*

Bridgewater. In contrast, 28.6 percent of the second year sample were diagnosed by Bridgewater as having some form of schizophrenia.

Construction and Analysis of the Competency Screening Test

The Competency Screening Test was developed using a sentence completion format. The sentence completion method has a long history in psychological assessment and has been found to be a valuable clinical and research approach that compares favorably in economy and power with other psychometric devices. (1, 2, 3, 4) The sentence completion format involves the construction of a list of beginning phrases (or sentence stems) and the development of a rationale for coding the wide range of responses that a sentence stem may elicit. Typical items included the following: "When Bob disagreed with his lawyer on his defense, he . . . ," "When I think of being sent to prison, I . . . ," and "If I had a chance to speak to the judge, I . . . " Administration takes about twenty-five minutes.

Beginning with fifty items, an early form of the Competency Screening Test was given to a wide range of competent and incompetent populations. The test was structured with the intent to focus on three kinds of items—those that represented the potential for a constructive relationship between the client and his lawyer — those that related to the understanding of the court process — and those that related to the ability to deal emotionally with the criminal process. On the basis of preliminary results, scoring techniques were defined and items that were not differentiated were eliminated.

The Competency Screening Test contains twenty-two items which are scored along integrated legal and psychological criteria. This produces a single score on each of the twenty-two items of 2 (competent), or 1 (questionable), or 0 (incompetent). Adequate interrater reliability was easily obtained (with raters at a bachelor degree level) with a brief period of training. Interrater reliability using standard Z scores was .93.

The next step in the analysis of the Competency Screening Test involved a factor analysis of its twenty-two individual items. The scores on these items obtained from the second and third year samples (N-91) were factor analyzed using a varimax orthogonal rotation.* Six rotated factors accounted for 56.3 percent of the total variance of the test (table I).

Factor 1 accounted for 19.5 percent of the common variance or communality explained by the six factors. This factor had the highest loading on items that clearly related to the dimension of the

---

*This rotation was based upon a set of factors whose original positions were determined by the Principle Components Factor Analysis program of the Data-Test System (Harvard Computing Center). The varimax rotation simplifies the columns of the factor matrix. The computing methods are based upon those suggested by Harman.[5] Standard "normalized" factor loadings were used in the rotations.

test that was intended to deal with the relationship of the defendant to his attorney in developing his defense. Factor 2, which accounted for 18.7 percent of the communality, showed the highest loading on those items that dealt with the defendant's understanding and awareness of the nature of the court process. Factor 3, which accounted for 18.8 percent of the communality, appeared to be parceling out that aspect of the defendant's responsiveness to the court process dealing with his reaction to accusation and guilt. This kind of responsiveness seems to deal with an affective or emotional level, in contrast to other aspects of competency that relate to cognitive capacities.

Factor 4, which accounted for 15.7 percent of the communality, included high loadings on items that could also be subsumed under the criterion of the defendant's understanding and awareness of the court process. However, some of these items with high loadings may reflect judgmental qualities in the defendant and his ability to participate in the strategy and evaluation required of one's own trial.

Factor 5, which accounted for 11.5 percent of the communality, showed high loadings on only two items; these reflected the defendant's trust and confidence in his lawyer. Factor 6, which accounted for 15.5 percent of the communality, had substantial loadings on those items that indicate a future orientation. In this respect, it seems to be related to that criterion of competency that focuses on the seriousness of the circumstances in which the defendant finds himself, or the peril of his position. The appropriateness of the planfulness of the defendant seems to be reflected in this factor.

A separate factor analysis was then conducted using scores on the Competency Screening Test obtained by a generally normal sample (N-83) containing no persons under observation for competency. The factors structure produced by this sample was markedly different from the factor structure produced by the Bridgewater samples. The clusters of factors did not produce any readily discernable concepts related to competency. The Competency Screening Test may thus be sample specific and may not measure competency in terms of the factors described above for populations differing from those of Bridgewater or populations not actively involved in the criminal justice system.

A further study of the Competency Screening Test was conducted using regression analyses, canonical correlations, and discriminant analyses with Bridgewater's recommendations regarding competency as the dependant or criterion variable. Regression analyses using various item scores, summed scores, and factor scores indicated five items that could be parsimoniously used to predict Bridgewater's findings. These five items were:

9. When the lawyer questioned his client in court, the client said
13. When the witness testifying against Harry gave incorrect

evidence, he

14. When Bob disagreed with his lawyer on his defense, he
19. When I think of being sent to prison, I
22. If I had a chance to speak to the judge, I

An examination of the factor matrix shows that item 9 loads on factors 3, 4, and 6; item 13 on factor 4; item 14 on factor 1; item 19 on factor 2; and item 22 on factor 6. Thus the patterns of factors and their related items on the Competency Screening Test appear to be related to the legal criteria of competency.*

Predictive Capabilities of the Competency Screening Test

Predictive accuracy has been further increased by combining items from standard tests with the Competency Screening Test. A step-wise discriminant analysis using two standard test items (Graham Kendall and Draw-a-Person Test — female) and four Competency Screening Tests items predicted competency findings with an overall accuracy of 93.1 percent** for the third year sample. (Table II)

Table II. Predictive Accuracy of the Competency Screening Test and Standard Test Items by Discriminant Analysis Using Court Determinations of Competency as the Criterion Variable

Court	Screening Test and Test Items	
	Competent	Incompetent
Competent	18	1
Incompetent	1	9

The Competency Screening Test alone or in combination with other tests does not predict with complete accuracy the competency recommendations of Bridgewater or the competency determinations of the court (literally synonymous with Bridgewater recommendations). An analysis of the "misclassified" cases (those cases in which Competency Screening Test predictions differ from court determinations) suggests that mentally deficient persons may tend to be considered competent by Bridgewater and the court when in fact their fitness for trial is in our opinion uncertain. Alternatively, some persons may be committed as incompetent who are fit for trial because they have exhibited behavior which is particularly disturbing to the community. A closer examination of

*This analysis is not meant to imply that these five CST items are the only useful items. A different pattern of items might emerge as equally useful for practical purposes, depending upon the sequence of the entry of the items into regression analyses.

**The six variables that best predicted compet ·.cy were (1) Graham Kendall, (2) Draw-a-Person Test (female), (3) "When the lawyer questioned his client in court, the client said," (4) "When Bob disagreed with his lawyer on his defense, he," (5) "When I think of being sent to prison, I," (6) "If I had chance to speak to the Judge, I". The major contribution came from the CST items. Weights of raw scores for the six variables were −0.03 (G-K), −0.08 (DAP), 0.45 (Lawyer), −0.55 (Bob), 0.63 (Prison), 0.30 (Speak).

those cases with high scores who were later committed as incompetent reveals that they tend to be persons who have a history of aggressive antisocial behavior and have deviated in a way that is especially repugnant to the community.*

Follow-up studies in which patients and their attorneys were interviewed following court hearings revealed a high level of agreement with Bridgewater recommendations, court findings, and CST predictions. Global ratings by attorneys as to whether they considered their defendants competent or incompetent were significantly related to both CST scores** and court determinations of competency.*** Although the attorneys were aware of the court determinations at the time of their rating, they were not aware of the CST scores previously received by their defendants. Thus, in this initial study, the CST appears to measure with reasonable accuracy the competency of defendants within the Massachusetts criminal justice system.

Relationship of the Competency Screening Test to Standard Tests

The total score received by each subject in the third year sample was compared with the scores he received on various scales on the Minnesota Multiphasic Personality Inventory (MMPI), the Wechsler Adult Intelligence Scale (WAIS), the Graham Kendall Memory for Design Test, the Draw-a-Person Test, and the Rorschach.[6] The testing on all of these items was done at the same time.

The following list shows the Pearson product-moment correlations between the Competency Screening Test total score and scores on standard test scales. Significant correlations are indicated.

CST Total Score

MMPI Lie Scale	0.132
MMPI Validity	-0.475++
Verbal IQ	0.150
Performance IQ	-0.073
Full Scale IQ	0.064
Graham Kendall Scale	-0.123
DAP Male	0.425+
DAP Female	0.325
DAP Self	0.064
Rorschach Empathy	0.044
Rorschach Hostility	0.224
Rorschach Dependency	0.065
Rorschach Body Preoccupation	0.081

---

*One case involved the murder by the patient of his child and one involved a sexual assault on a child. Another case involved disturbing the peace, a relatively nonserious offense from a legal point of view; however, this disturbance involved a threat to kill a police officer.

**Fisher Exact Test = 0.02; phi = 0.61.

***Fisher Exact Test = 0.02; phi = 0.59.

CST Total Score—Continued

Rorschach Repression   0.399+

  + = .05

  ++ = .01

BIBLIOGRAPHY

1. Fiske, D.W., and Van Buskirk, C. The stability of interpretation of sentence completion tests. *J Consult Psychol*, 23:170–180, 1959.
2. Goldberg, P.A. A review of sentence completion methods in personality assessment. *J Project Techn*, 29:12–45, 1965.
3. Rotter, J.B., and Willerman, B. The incomplete sentences test as a method of studying personality. *J Consult Psychol*, 11:43–48, 1947.
4. Karen, R.L. A method for rating sentence completion test responses. *J Project Techn*, 25:312–314, 1961.
5. Herman, H.H. *Modern Factor Analysis*. Chicago, Ill.: Univ. of Chicago Press, 1964.
6. Pruitt, W., and Spilka, B. Rorschach empathy-object relationship scale. *J Project Techn*, 16:133–150, 1952.

APPENDIX B

COMPETENCY TO STAND TRIAL
ASSESSMENT INSTRUMENT AND HANDBOOK

COMPETENCY TO STAND TRIAL ASSESSMENT INSTRUMENT

	Total	Severe	Moderate	Mild	None	Unratable
			Degree of Incapacity			
1. Appraisal of available legal defenses	1	2	3	4	5	6
2. Unmanageable behavior	1	2	3	4	5	6
3. Quality of relating to attorney	1	2	3	4	5	6
4. Planning of legal strategy, including guilty plea to lesser charges where pertinent	1	2	3	4	5	6
5. Appraisal of role of: a. Defense counsel	1	2	3	4	5	6
b. Prosecuting attorney	1	2	3	4	5	6
c. Judge	1	2	3	4	5	6
d. Jury	1	2	3	4	5	6
e. Defendant	1	2	3	4	5	6
f. Witnesses	1	2	3	4	5	6
6. Understanding of court procedure	1	2	3	4	5	6
7. Appreciation of charges	1	2	3	4	5	6
8. Appreciation of range and nature of possible penalties	1	2	3	4	5	6
9. Appraisal of likely outcome	1	2	3	4	5	6
10. Capacity to disclose to attorney available pertinent facts surrounding the offense including the defendant's movements, timing, mental state, actions at the time of the offense	1	2	3	4	5	6
11. Capacity to realistically challenge prosecution witnesses	1	2	3	4	5	6
12. Capacity to testify relevantly	1	2	3	4	5	6
13. Self-defeating v. self-serving motivation (legal sense)	1	2	3	4	5	6

Examinee _____ Examiner _____

Date _____

COMPETENCY TO STAND TRIAL: ASSESSMENT INSTRUMENT

I. Introduction

The instrument which this code book describes was designed to improve communication between the behavioral science disciplines (particularly psychiatry) and the law in an area of mutual responsibility — the determination of competency to stand trial. Prior attempts at such communication have suffered from the understandable tendency of each of these disciplines to adhere to the language and concepts of their own discipline. Thus the findings of the clinician have not been delivered in a form and language which are appropriate to the needs of the court. Insofar as clinical opinion has been delivered to the courts in this area, it has tended to be global, conclusional, and not substantiated by relevant clinical data.

We sought, therefore, to develop an instrument which delivered clinical opinion to the court in language, form, and substance sufficiently common to the disciplines involved to provide a basis for adequate and relevant communication. The purpose of the instrument is to standardize, objectify, and quantify the relevant criteria for competency to stand trial.

II. The Instrument

The instrument may be described as a series of thirteen functions related to an accused's ability to cope with the trial process in an adequately self-protective fashion. These functions or items were culled from appellate cases, the legal literature, and our clinical and courtroom experience. The total series is intended to cover all possible grounds for a finding of incompetency. The weight which the court may be expected to assign to one or another of the items will not be equal, nor is it intended to be. Neither will the weight assigned to a given item by the court in reaching a finding on competency for a particular defendant necessarily apply to the next defendant. For example, in the court's view, it may be far more critical to the defense of a particular defendant that he be able to "testify relevantly" than for another defendant whose attorney does not intend to put him on the stand. Considerations of the weight to be assigned a given item in the case of a particular defendant goes beyond the scope of what should be expected of the examining clinician. The task for the clinician is the providing of objective data, the import of which is the responsibility of the court.

This instrument is designed to reflect the competency status of a defendant at the time of examination. It is not a predictive instrument. Our experience indicates that with the passage of time and variations in clinical status, even from day to day, a given defendant will vary in the scores attained. This is particularly true of patient-defendants recovering from an acute psychosis.

It is important to note at the onset that the inability to function indicated by low scores on this instrument must arise from mental illness and/or mental retardation and not, for example, from ideological motivation. When there is doubt as to its connection with abnormal and mental processes, the item should not be scored and it should be indicated that the opinion does not reach reasonable clinical certainty on the particular item.

At the very least, individual items which are scored at one or two (out of a scale of five) should be substantiated by diagnostic and clinical data of adequate richness to establish a serious degree of mental illness or retardation and the manner in which such disability relates to the low degree of functioning in the particular item.

It should be noted that defendants with mental disability of a serious degree, including psychosis and moderate mental retardation, frequently are quite competent and may achieve high scores on any or all of the items. Mental disability is relevant to a competency determination only insofar as it is manifested by malfunctioning in one or more of the specific items of the instrument.

In the scoring of this instrument a basic assumption is that the accused will be adequately aided by counsel. A second basic assumption is that the professional who is using this instrument has at least a basic understanding of and experience in the realities of the criminal justice system.

Each item in the instrument is scaled from 1 to 5 ranging from "total incapacity" at one to "no incapacity" at five. If the instrument is used for outpatient or incourt screening purposes, a majority or a substantial accumulation of scores of three or lower in the thirteen items could be regarded as grounds for a period of inpatient observation and more intensive workup.

In our experience with patient-defendants who are in good contact, the examination and scoring, using this instrument, usually does not require more than one hour. Grossly psychotic or passive, concrete and under-responsive defendants obviously may require more extended examination. Care should be taken not to resort to leading questions. The device of offering two or three alternative choices to such defendants has been found to be useful.

100

In using this instrument interrater reliability can be significantly enhanced by frequent reference to the brief definitions of each item which follow in Section III of this code book. Section IV provides expanded definitions, an interview protocol and brief clinical examples of defendants functioning at different levels of each of the thirteen items. Section V contains a summary of the studies of interrater reliability completed prior to the general dissemination of the instrument.

A score of *one* on the instrument indicates that for the item scored a close to or total lack of capacity to function exists of the order of a mute or incoherent person or a severe retardate.

A score of *two* indicates that for the item scored there is severely impaired functioning and a substantial question of adequacy for the particular function.

A score of *three* indicates that there is moderately impaired functioning and a question of adequacy for the particular function.

A score of *four* indicates that for the item scored there is mildly impaired functioning and little question of adequacy for the particular function. An individual can be mildly impaired on the basis of lack of experience in the legal process or sociocultural deprivation with or without attendant psychic pathology.

A score of *five* indicates that for the item scored there is no impairment and no question that the defendant can function adequately for the particular function.

A score of *six* indicates that the available data do not permit a rating which is within reasonable clinical certainty.

III. Brief Definitions

1. *Appraisal of available legal defenses:* This item calls for an assessment of the accused's awareness of his possible legal defenses and how consistent these are with the reality of his particular circumstances.

2. *Unmanageable behavior:* This item calls for an assessment of the appropriateness of the current motor and verbal behavior of the defendant and the degree to which this behavior would disrupt the conduct of a trial. Inappropriate or disruptive behavior must arise from a substantial degree of mental illness or mental retardation.

3. *Quality of relating to attorney:* This item calls for an assessment of the interpersonal capacity of the accused to relate to the average attorney. Involved are the ability to trust and to communicate relevantly.

4. *Planning of legal strategy including guilty pleas to lesser charges where pertinent:* This item calls for an assessment of the degree to which the accused can understand, participate, and cooperate with his counsel in planning a strategy for the defense which is consistent with the reality of his circumstances.

5. *Appraisal of role of:* a. Defense counsel
                       b. Prosecuting attorney
                       c. Judge
                       d. Jury
                       e. Defendant
                       f. Witnesses

This set of items calls for a minimal understanding of the adversary process by the accused. The accused should be able to identify prosecuting attorney and prosecution witnesses as foe, defense counsel as friend, the judge as neutral, and the jury as the determiners of guilt or innocence.

6. *Understanding of court procedure:* This item calls for an assessment of the degree to which the defendant understands the basic sequence of events in a trial and their import for him; e.g., the different purposes of direct and cross examination.

7. *Appreciation of charges:* This item calls for an assessment of the accused's understanding of the charges against him and, to a lesser extent, the seriousness of the charges.

8. *Appreciation of range and nature of possible penalties:* This item calls for an assessment of the accused's concrete understanding and appreciation of the conditions and restrictions which could be imposed on him and their possible duration.

9. *Appraisal of likely outcome:* This item calls for an assessment of how realistically the accused perceives the likely outcome and the degree to which impaired understanding contributes to a less adequate or inadequate participation in his defense. Without adequate information on the part of the examiner regarding the facts and circumstances of the alleged offense, this item would be unratable.

10. *Capacity to disclose to attorney available pertinent facts surrounding the offense including the defendant's movements, timing, mental state, and actions at the time of the offense:* This item calls for an assessment of the accused's capacity to give a basically consistent, rational, and relevant account of the motivational and external facts. Complex factors can enter into this determination. These include intelligence, memory, and honesty. The difficult area of the validity of an amnesia may be involved and may prove unresolvable for the examining clinician. It is important to be aware that there may be a disparity between what an accused is willing to share with a clinician as opposed to what he will share with his attorney, the latter being the more important.

11. *Capacity to realistically challenge prosecution witnesses:* This item calls for an assessment of the accused's capacity to recognize distortions in prosecution testimony. Relevant factors include attentiveness and memory. In addition, there is an element of initiative in that if false testimony is given, the degree of activism

with which the defendant will apprise his attorney of inaccuracies, is of importance.

12. *Capacity to testify relevantly:* This item calls for an assessment of the accused's ability to testify with coherence, relevance, and independence of judgment.

13. *Self-defeating v. self-serving motivation (legal sense):* This item calls for an assessment of the accused's motivation to adequately protect himself and appropriately utilize legal safeguards to this end. It is recognized that accused persons may appropriately be motivated to seek expiation and appropriate punishment in their trials. At issue here is the pathological seeking of punishment and the deliberate failure by the accused to avail himself of appropriate legal portections. Passivity or indifference do not justify low scores on this item. Actively self-destructive manipulation of the legal process arising from mental pathology does justify low scores.

IV. Expanded Definitions with Sample Interview Questions and Clinical Examples

1. *Appraisal of available legal defenses:* This item calls for an assessment of the accused's awareness of his possible legal defenses, and how consistent these are with the reality of his particular circumstances.

Questions such as the following will yield data relevant to the scoring of this item:

How do you think you can be defended against these charges?
How can you explain your way out of these charges?
What do you think your lawyer should concentrate on in order to best defend you?

Clinical examples: An elderly paranoid man charged with assault and battery with a dangerous weapon (a golf club) on a neighbor, utterly denied that any attack had taken place and indicated that the "CIA had put him (i.e., the neighbor) up to it." He was unable to offer or agree to any alternative possibility of a defense. He received a score of 2, indicating severely impaired functioning and a substantial question of adequacy for this item.

A retired sailor living alone on inherited property is accused of murder. The victim was a young boy who was among a group of boys throwing stones at the defendant's house at the time of the alleged offense. The defendant reported that he had complained often to the local police about repeated harassments but that they ignored him. He further reported that he had written to the F.B.I., the U.S. Attorney General, and other authorities with no response. Although when he fired the shot he stated that he had shot over the heads of the boys, his theory of his proper defense was that a man in this country had the "inviolable constitutional right to protect his property with a gun," and he insisted that he would instruct his attorney to proceed with a defense only on this basis. Although insisting on his theory of defense, he did agree that his intent to fire over the heads of the boys should be put in evidence but that it was incidental to the main defense. He received a score of 3, indicating moderately impaired functioning and a question of his adequacy on this item.

A middle-aged man with a long history of criminal arrests, mostly for drunkenness, had been found guilty in lower court of four counts of larceny from his 83-year-old girl friend of a total sum exceeding $16,000. He received four sentences of two years each in the County House of Correction to be served "on and after," a total of eight years. His lawyer appealed and a new trial in the Superior Court had been scheduled. When interviewed, the defendant proved to be concrete, passive, and under-responsive. When asked the basis of his appeal he answered several times, "I don't know, my lawyer has all the facts." When offered the speculation that the lawyer may have appealed either on a legal technicality or because the sentence was too severe, the defendant answered, "He thinks it's too long. I hope to get two or three years." Later in the interview he stated that his girl friend was lying and that she had given him the money to "play the horses," and that she "was there," i.e., at the race track. However, he stated, "They wouldn't believe me because of my record." He received a score of 4, indicating mild incapacity and little question of adequacy on this item.

2. *Unmanageable behavior:* This item calls for an assessment of the appropriateness of the current motor and verbal behavior of the defendant, and the degree to which this behavior would disrupt the conduct of a trial. Inappropriate or disruptive behavior must arise from a substantial degree of mental illness or mental retardation.

For this item, obviously observations as to the patient's manifest behavior are relevant and the content of the answers to questions less relevant. Questions we have used and found useful follow:

Do you realize that you would have to control yourself in the courtroom and not interrupt the proceedings?

When is the only time you can speak out in the courtroom?

What do you think would happen if you spoke out or moved around in the courtroom without permission?

Clinical examples: A young, male adult paranoid schizophrenic on two occasions (his arraignment and an earlier competency hearing) interrupts his attorney and addresses the court in loud tones, dismissing his attorney and insisting on voicing paranoid delusions to the effect that his attorney is part of a conspiracy by the F.B.I. to put him in prison because he is falsely believed to be a presidential assassin. On one occasion he struggled with court officers in an attempt to put "a petition to dismiss," which he had written, on the judge's desk. He was given a score of 2, indicating severely impaired functioning and a substantial question of adequacy on this item.

A manic defendant, although responsive to questions and in contact, is unable to remain seated during an examination for more than a few moments and moves distractedly about the room, lifting objects, pacing, rapping the walls. He received a score of 3, indicating that there is moderately impaired functioning and a question of adequacy for this item.

During the examination, a chronic schizophrenic, repeatedly grimaces, raises his right hand with three fingers extended, then places his index finger against his right temple. This recurs whether he is speaking or not. His hand is at rest only when he places it inside the belt of his pants. He was given a score of 4, indicating mildly impaired functioning and little question of adequacy on this item.

3. *Quality of relating to attorney:* This item calls for an assessment of the interpersonal capacity of the accused to relate to the average attorney. Involved are the ability to trust and to communicate relevantly.

The degree of trust and relevancy of communication which the defendant manifests with an examining psychiatrist is applicable here up to a point. Usually the defendant will have had at least one contact with his defense counsel and the questions we have found useful with this item are as follows:

Do you have confidence in your lawyer?

Do you think he's trying to do a good job for you?

Do you agree with the way he's handled or plans to handle your case?

Clinical examples: A middle-aged defendant with a diagnosis of involutional paranoid state is accused of killing a childhood acquaintance of his wife. He refused to see his court-appointed attorney and insists on handling his defense himself. His theory of defense consists of a claim of self-defense in that he and the victim struggled for possession of a gun and in the struggle the victim was shot accidentally four times. "I don't trust lawyers. They're all part of the criminal system. I'm going to tell my side of the story in my own way." He received a score of 2, indicating a severely impaired functioning and a substantial question of adequacy for this item.

A defendant is accused of the murder of his wife. He is cooperative with his attorney but insists, against the attorney's advice, that he will take the stand in order to tell "my side of the story." This consists of his continuing delusion that his wife had been poisoning his food and that this had resulted in his becoming impotent and "like a zombie." He received a score of 3, indicating moderately impaired functioning and a question of adequacy for this item.

A seventeen-year-old depressed black accused of assault and battery with a dangerous weapon is asked, "Do you have a lawyer?" and answers, "No, I have a public defender." When asked, "Do you have confidence in him?" he answered, "I don't know yet. I don't think he's very interested in my case." He received a score of 4, indicating mild incapacity and little question of adequacy on this item.

4. *Planning of legal strategy including guilty pleas to lesser charges where pertinent:* This item calls for an assessment of the degree to which the accused can understand, participate, and cooperate with his counsel in planning a strategy for the defense which is consistent with the reality of his circumstances.

Most frequently the issue here relates to plea-bargaining and agreement to settle for a guilty plea to a lesser offense. Less frequently strategic issues such as a change of venue, consideration of a plea of not guilty by reason of insanity, or the decision as to whether or not defendant should testify, arise and require some participation from the defendant. The essential question is whether or not the defendant can join with his attorney, even if passively, in planning (or accepting) appropriate legal strategy. Of concern here is the defendant who insists on irrational instructions to his attorney or insists on defending himself on the basis of an irrational theory of defense. Questions which have been useful on this issue are as follows:

If your lawyer can get the District Attorney to accept a guilty plea to (manslaughter) instead of trying you for (murder — use examples relevant to the actual case, e.g., trespassing in place of breaking and entry, etc.) would you agree to it?

If your lawyer decides not to have you testify would you go along with him?

Is there anything that you disagree with in the way your lawyer is going to handle your case, and if so, what do you plan to do about it?

Clinical examples: A grandiose, acute schizophrenic is accused of illegal possession of a fire arm. The defense attorney confers with the lower court judge who agrees to continue the case without a finding on the understanding that defendant would accept mental hospitalization. The defendant is willing to accept hospitalization but insists on a trial and "appeal all the way to the Supreme Court to expose the Fascist state we live in. I am L-4-C." He was given a score of 2, indicating severely impaired functioning and a substantial question of adequacy for this item.

An impotent man stabs his twelve-year-old daughter to death while she stands beside his bed because he "sensed evil in her that was rotting my life." He states that he would refuse to plead guilty to manslaughter if it could be arranged and insists on a trial for murder and "No lawyer would ever talk me out of it." He received a score of 3, indicating moderately impaired functioning and a question of his adequacy on this item.

A mental retardate with an I.Q. of 66 is accused of a homicide. He is highly suggestible and passive. His trust and dependency are easily obtained but he is capable of little or no independence of judgment and places himself uncritically and totally in the hands of his attorney. He received a score of 4, indicating mild incapacity and little question of adequacy on this item.

5. *Appraisal of role of:* a. Defense counsel
                             b. Prosecuting attorney
                             c. Judge
                             d. Jury
                             e. Defendant
                             f. Witnesses

This set of items calls for a minimal understanding of the adversary process by the accused. The accused should be able to identify prosecuting attorney and prosecution witnesses as foe, defense counsel as friend, the judge as neutral, and the jury as the determiners of guilt or innocence.

For this item a single question generally suffices and that is: *In the courtroom during a trial, what is the job of* . . . . (here list the sub-items)? It is particularly relevant that the defendant be aware of the purposes of the prosecuting attorney.

Clinical examples: A young adult retardate (I.Q. 67) was asked "What is the job of the district attorney in court?" He answered, "He's a lawyer. Lawyers are supposed to help people." The defendant was then instructed about the actual role of the prosecutor, but on subsequent questioning it was clear that he was still unable to conceptualize the prosecutorial functions of the district attorney. He was given a score of 2, indicating that there was severely impaired functioning and a substantial question of adequacy for this sub-item.

When asked the job of defense counsel in court, a chronic paranoid schizophrenic with a fourth grade education, answered "My own lawyer is supposed to help the law." He was then asked, "And you too?" to which he answered, "Yes, a little." He was given a score of 3 on the "defense attorney" sub-item indicating moderately impaired functioning and a question of adequacy.

When asked about the job of the district attorney a poorly educated black who recently settled in Boston after an upbringing in the South, answered, "He's there to get out the truth." He was given a score of 4, indicating mildly impaired functioning, but with little question of adequacy on the "prosecuting attorney" sub-item.

6. *Understanding of court procedure:* This item calls for an assessment of the degree to which the defendant understands the basic sequence of events in a trial and their import for him, e.g., the different purposes of direct and cross examination.

An understanding of procedural niceties is not required here. Questions we have used to elicit relevant data here are as follows:

Who is the only one at your trial who can call on you to testify?

After your lawyer finished asking you questions on the stand, who then can ask you questions?

If the District Attorney (prosecutor) asks you questions, what is he trying to accomplish?

Clinical examples: A young adult, white, grandiose paranoid schizophrenic accused of indecent assault and battery on a minor refused counsel and insisted that he would conduct his own defense. He stated, "I will ask the questions. I will call the district attorney to the stand and expose their criminal black conspiracy against me." He received a score of 2, indicating severely impaired functioning and a substantial question of adequacy on the "defendant" sub-item.

A mildly retarded adult male (I.Q. 66) with a prior record of misdemeanors disposed of in lower court is charged with his first felony, breaking and entry in the nighttime. He states, "The judge will ask me questions to try to find out the truth. The lawyers are there to help me. They will ask questions, too." Attempts by the interviewer to explain the role of the district attorney in cross examination are met with partial success. The defendant subsequently states, "I understand that if the district attorney asks me questions he's trying to send me to jail." He received a score of 3, indicating moderately impaired functioning and a question of adequacy on this item.

A middle-aged man diagnosed as an inadequate personality is charged with incest. It is his first experience with criminal prosecution. He states, "I don't know anything about the law. I suppose my lawyer will take care of me. Yes, I used to watch Perry Mason." He was given a score of 4, indicating mildly impaired functioning and little question of adequacy on this item.

7. *Appreciation of charges:* This item calls for an assessment of the accused's concrete understanding of the charges against him, and to a lesser extent the seriousness of the charges.

What is required here should be exaggerated. Basically a literal knowledge of the specific charge or charges is adequate. An understanding of the seriousness of the charges is of importance here only insofar as it might contribute to a perhaps cavalier or indifferent cooperation by the defendant in his defense. For example, if a manic defendant views an arson, as a lark and is disposed to freely admit his action, there is question as to his self-protective capacity on this item. Questions useful in eliciting data here are:

What are you charged with?

Is that a major or a minor charge?

Do you think people in general would regard you with some fear on the basis of such a charge?

Clinical examples: A 19-year-old retardate (I.Q. 55) is accused of statutory rape of a 12-year-old girl. When asked why the police arrested him he smirks and waves his finger back and forth saying "No-no." When asked how old the girl was he says, "Not know, big girl." In an effort to establish the victim's age and sexual maturity in the defendant's eyes, pictures are drawn giving the defendant a choice between side views of women with very small, medium, and large breasts. With a mischievous and naughty facial expression he touches the picture with the very small breasts. He was given a score of 2, indicating severely impaired functioning and a substantial question of adequacy on this item.

A young adult catatonic schizophrenic is accused of arson of a church. When asked what he is accused of he states, "started a fire." When asked the seriousness of the charge, he answers, "No harm . . . (moan) stone won't burn." He was given a score of 3, indicating moderately impaired functioning and a question of adequacy on this item.

A manic defendant accused of successfully forging checks in the amount of $7,500 states, "They can't touch me. Any day now I'll be on the big board at the stock exchange. I'll cover the checks." He was given a score of 4, indicating mildly impaired functioning and little question of adequacy on this item.

8. *Appreciation of range and nature of possible penalties:* This item calls for an assessment of the accused's concrete understanding and appreciation of the conditions and restrictions which could be imposed on him and their possible duration.

Here, too, a concrete, simplistic understanding suffices. Generally, if the crime is a felony, the defendant should be aware that there is at least a potential state prison sentence even if such a sentence is unlikely in his circumstances. The potential sentence need not be know with precision. Of concern here is that the defendant have at least a gross understanding of what is at risk and a motivation to protect himself which is consistent with the risk. Relevant questions here are:

> If you're found guilty as charged what are the possible sentences the judge could give you?
> Where would you have to serve such a sentence?
> If you're put on probation, what does that mean?

Clinical examples: A 19-year-old retardate (I.Q. 55) accused of statutory rape states, "No jail, me go home to mother." He was given a score of 2, indicating severely impaired functioning and a substantial question of adequacy on this item.

An elderly retired school teacher who had recently been widowed is accused of indecent assault and battery on the 7-year-old daughter of a neighbor. His diagnosis is senile dementia. He is irascible and insists that he simply "petted" the girl and that "no further prosecution is appropriate" and that there is no possibility of incarceration for such an "act" and "jail is for rapists and revolutionaries." He received a score of 3, indicating a moderately impaired functioning and a question of adequacy on this item.

A paranoid young woman who blames the mother of a former boyfriend for their breakup forces her way into the apartment of the mother. During an ensuing argument she picks up a poker and threatens the mother. The police are called and she is physically subdued. She is accused of attempted assault and battery with a dangerous weapon, breaking and entering in the nighttime, and resisting arrest. She states, "I suppose it's possible that they could send me to jail, but it's inconceivable. I've calmed down now. I will not further dignify that woman by responding to her trumped-up charges. The burden of these proceedings rests with her." She received a score of 4, indicating mild incapacity and little question of her adequacy on this item.

9. *Appraisal of likely outcome:* This item calls for an assessment of how realistically the accused perceives the likely outcome, and the degree to which impaired understanding contributes to a less adequate or inadequate participation in his defense. Without adequate information on the part of the examiner regarding the facts and circumstances of the alleged offense, this item would be unratable.

A police arrest report and/or communication from defense counsel or district attorney as to the real facts and circumstances surrounding the alleged offense are helpful here. If the patient irrationally perceives that there is little or no peril in his position and the case against him is strong, it might follow that he would have little or no motivation to adequately protect himself. Here, also, the psychotic person who, for irrational reasons, does not accept the criminal jurisdiction of the court might not adequately protect himself. Questions were used as follows:

What do you think your chances are to be found not guilty?
Does the court you're going to be tried in have authority over you?
How strong a case do they have against you?

Clinical examples: A middle-aged man diagnosed as involutional paranoid state is accused of the murder of his wife. He states, "This was an act of God. No temporal power has any authority over me. I will not participate in these proceedings." He was given a score of 2, indicating severely impaired functioning and a substantial question of adequacy on this item.

A paranoid young woman who blames the mother of a former boyfriend for their breakup forces her way into the apartment of his mother. During an ensuing argument she picks up a poker and threatens the mother. The police are called and she is physically subdued by them. She is accused of attempted assault and battery with a dangerous weapon, breaking and entering in the nighttime and resisting arrest. She states, "I suppose it's possible that they could send me to jail but it's inconceivable. I've calmed down now. I will not further dignify that woman by responding to her trumped-up charges. The burden of these proceedings rests with her." She received a score of 3, indicating moderately impaired functioning and a question of adequacy on this item.

A schizoid 20-year-old son of wealthy parents is accused of grand larceny from a mail order firm where he had worked as a shipping clerk. He states, "My father has hired the best lawyer in town for me. I don't have to lift a finger in there (i.e., the courtroom). The worst I could get is probation." He was given a score of 4, indicating mild incapacity and little question of adequacy on this item.

10. *Capacity to disclose to attorney available pertinent facts surrounding the offense including the defendant's movements, timing, mental state, and actions at the time of the offense:* This item calls for an assessment of the accused's capacity to give a basically consistent, rational, and relevant account of the motivational and external facts. Complex factors can enter into this determination. These include intelligence, memory, and honesty. The difficult area of the validity of an amnesia may be involved and may prove unresolvable for the examiner. It is important to be aware that there may be a disparity between what an accused is willing to share with a clinician and what he will share with his attorney; the latter being the more important.

It is assumed that answers to questions on this item will not be available to the prosecution for purposes of incrimination and will be limited to the narrow question of the accused's competency. Here, too, the examiner should have adequate knowledge of the facts of the alleged offense from the police arrest report or counsel in order to record a valid score. Relevant questions are:

> Tell us what actually happened, what you saw and did and heard and thought before, during, and after you are supposed to have committed this offense.
>
> When and where did all this take place?
>
> What led the police to arrest you and what did you say to them?

Clinical examples: The alleged driver of a bank robbery getaway car is accused of armed robbery. In a high speed chase following the robbery an accident occurs and the defendant suffers a fractured skull and is unconscious for 12 hours. After emergency surgery for an epidural hematoma, the defendant complains of a retrograde amnesia from the time of the accident. He further asserts that he does not know his alleged confederate and states, "He must have made me drive at the point of a gun, but I don't remember." He was given a score of 2, indicating severely impaired functioning and a substantial question of adequacy on this item.

A State police sergeant 10 years from retirement is involved in a harrowing ghetto riot. His patrol car is surrounded by a mob which overturns the car while he is in it. He is subsequently rescued unhurt. Two weeks later, while driving home after a period of duty, he has an abrupt amnestic episode. Several hours later he is arrested by fellow police officers in a suburban home with a stolen car outside the home and two neighbors hand-cuffed to a pipe. He claims an amnesia except for isolated flashbacks. "I remember a scene with two people hand-cuffed to a pipe. I don't remember how I got there. The rest is blank. I last remember being on the freeway with my car." He was diagnosed hysterical neurosis, dissociative type and given a score of 3, indicating moderate incapacity and a question of adequacy on this item.

A 50-year-old catatonic schizophrenic is indicted for murder for the second time in his life. On the first occasion he was found not guilty by reason of insanity and subsequently released. He has been hospitalized for 10 years since the second alleged murder after having been found incompetent to stand trial. He is now in a stable remission from his illness on thorazine and wants to stand trial. On examination he states, "He (the victim) was a friend. We were in the kitchen. He leaned down to pick up something. I picked up the ax and hit him. I didn't plan it. It just happened. I didn't have any feelings." He was given a score of 4, indicating mild incapacity and little question of adequacy on this item.

11. *Capacity to realistically challenge prosecution witnesses:* This item calls for an assessment of the accused's capacity to recognize distortions in prosecution testimony. Relevant factors include attentiveness and memory. In addition there is an element of initiative. If false testimony is given the degree of activism with which the defendant will apprise his attorney of inaccuracies is important.

The relevant considerations turn primarily on the observations of the examiner regarding the perceptual abilities of the defendant during the clinical examination rather than on the content of answers to questions. Questions we have used are:

Suppose a witness against you told a lie in the courtroom. What would you do?

Is there anybody who is likely to tell lies about you in this case? Why?

Clinical examples: An elderly, paranoid man attacks his neighbor with a golf club. He is accused of assault and battery with a dangerous weapon. "The whole thing's a lie," he said. "If he (the neighbor) testifies I will stand up and tell the jury that he is a C.I.A. agent and that he is in a conspiracy against me. I will not allow him to testify." He received a score of 2, indicating severe incapacity and a substantial question of adequacy on this item.

A skid row alcoholic with organic deterioration is accused of breaking and entering and larceny. He states, "I don't remember things too good. Let them have it (i.e., the prosecution witnesses) their way. I was drunk. I don't remember taking anything." He was given a score of 3, indicating moderate incapacity and a question of adequacy on this item.

A mildly retarded (I.Q. 67) young, adult male who is passive and under-responsive, answers, "I don't know," to the question, "What would you do if a witness told a lie about you in the courtroom?" He is then advised that he should quietly get his lawyer's attention in such a situation and inform him of the lie. On subsequent questioning he shows that he has understood and that he would tell his lawyer. He received a score of 4, indicating mild incapacity and little question of adequacy on this item.

112

12. *Capacity to testify relevantly:* This item calls for an assessment of the accused's ability to testify with coherence, relevance, and independence of judgment.

Here again the relevant data arise primarily from the observations of the examiner regarding the defendant's ability to verbally communicate rather then sepcific content in the answers to specific questions. Affective as well as thought disorder considerations are of some relevance here, e.g., if the defendant is immobilized by anxiety or depression, or is manic, loose or regressed in his associations and responses. If questions, which might come up in direct and cross examination of the defendant, can be anticipated, given the facts and circumstances of the particular case, then this would of course be helpful but it is not essential for a valid rating on this item.

Clinical examples: A 40-year-old, homeless male diagnosed as a simple schizophrenic breaks into a rural food store. He eats some of the food in the store and then goes to sleep. In the morning the proprietor finds him. He is arrested and charged with breaking and entering and larceny. On being interviewed there are long pauses before he can answer questions and they must be repeated gently. "I had no money ... I was hungry ... I was cold ... I went to sleep." He was given a score of 2, indicating severe incapacity and a substantial question of adequacy on this item.

A 30-year-old male schizophrenic (chronic undifferentiated type) is arrested after neighbors report that he has been shooting out of his window at dogs in his back yard. He is accused of illegal posession and unlawful discharge of a firearm. He insists on being tried to "clear the record" and refuses the alternative of mental hospitalization. He states that he was trying to "scare off" the dogs and had no intention of "hitting" them. However, he continues to talk after these objective answers to questions and rambles in a loosely associated, tangential, and circumstantial manner. He resists any interruptions in his discourses but can be stopped with some effort. He received a score of 3, indicating moderate incapacity and a question of adequacy on this item.

A mildly retarded young man (I.Q. 60) is accused, in his terms, of "first degree murder." He is concrete in his answers and has a very limited vocabulary. When pressed to elaborate on his answers or when vocabulary is used which he does not understand, he retreats to "I don't know." He can, given his limitations, nevertheless give an accurate and consistent, if simplistic, story of the events surrounding the alleged offense. He was given a score of 4, indicating mild incapacity and little question of adequacy on this item.

13. *Self-defeating v. self-serving motivation (legal sense):* This item calls for an assessment of the accused's motivation to adequately protect himself and appropriately utilize legal safeguards to this end. It is recognized that accused persons may appropriately

be motivated to seek expiation and appropriate punishment in their trials. Of concern here is the pathological seeking of punishment and the deliberate failure by the accused to avail himself of appropriate legal protections. Passivity or indifference do not justify low scores on this item. Actively self-destructive manipulation of the legal process arising from mental pathology does justify low scores.

In this item the issue turns on the willingness of the accused to take advantage of appropriate *legal* protections even though he may feel that he should be punished. Will he, in other words, play the game; taking advantage of the rules built into the system for his portection. Relevant questions:

> We know how badly you feel about what happened — suppose your lawyer is successful in getting you off — would you accept that?

> Suppose the District Attorney made some legal errors and your lawyer wants to appeal a guilty finding in your case — would you accept that?

> We know that you want to plead guilty to your charge — but what if you lawyer could get the District Attorney to agree to a plea of guilty to a lesser charge — would you accept that?

Clinical examples: A 33-year-old paranoid schizophrenic is accused of murder. He is convinced that he will and should be executed since his is the "second messianic crucifixion." He declines a negotiated plea of manslaughter and attempts to instruct his attorney not to call any defense witnesses. He intends to address the court to request the death sentence since he "owes this to sinning mankind." He received a score of 2, indicating severely impaired functioning and a substantial question of adequacy for this item.

A middle-aged, unemployed house painter is accused of the murder of his eight-year-old daughter. At the time of the homicide, the defendant was convinced that the "end of the world" had come and that the "forces of the devil were at loose in the world," and that they were coming to "rape and murder my daughter." He was convinced he had to kill her to "be sure she would enter heaven without sin." After the homicide he is convinced that the devil had "taken over my body" but that he now "must make expiation." He insists on pleading guilty to first degree murder and he will be satisfied at nothing less than a "life sentence." He received a score of 3, indicating moderately impaired functioning and a question of adequacy on this item.

A chronic paranoid schizophrenic adult male with prior prison sentences sets a fire and turns himself into the police. He states, "I can't make it on the outside. They won't admit me at the State Hospital. I've got to get away for a while. I'd like to get 2 or 3 years." He received a score of 4, indicating mild incapacity and little question of adequacy on this item.

V. Inter-rater Reliability and the Validity of the Instrument

Experienced staff of the project that developed the Competency Assessment Instrument achieved a high reliability coefficient (.92) according to intraclass R analysis. This analysis was based on multiple observer assessments of 18 patient-defendants at the Bridgewater State Hospital and the Suffolk Superior Court (felony jurisdiction) in Boston. A technique of recording assessments followed by feedback and consensus seeking with frequent reference to this *Handbook*, particularly Section III (Brief Definitions), appeared to be responsible for the development of high reliability coefficients. Three observers having little or no previous experience in the competency area assessed at least five of the 18 patients at the same time. The first patient received a reliability coefficient of .64, but utilizing the *Handbook* consensus seeking, the score increased to .87. It also appeared to be important in developing high interrater reliability to adhere strictly to the structured interview protocol recorded in Section IV of the *Handbook* (Expanded Definitions with Sample Interview Questions and Clinical Examples).

Subsequently, 216 clinicians in Massachusetts from several disciplines (psychiatry, psychology, social work and nursing), some of whom had studied the *Handbook*, achieved an overall reliability coefficient of 0.84 in assessing patient-defendants. The 216 observers rated 13 different patient-defendants in eight sessions at seven State hospitals in Massachusetts. Reliability coefficients were arrived at using randomly selected cohorts of three observors. Larger cohorts produce falsely high reliability coefficients in intraclass R analyses (Haggard 1968). Three of the project staff who were experienced with the instrument rated the same patients and arrived at a reliability coefficient of .89.

Some caution should be expressed here, since certain sub-groups of the 216 observers had relatively low reliability coefficients. For example, although observers who had an opportunity to study the *Handbook* prior to the examination had higher reliability (R of .84) than those who did not (R of .72), those who studied the *Handbook* for more than one hour tended to have a greater mean divergence from the scores of experienced project staff. Also, those with either very little experience or a great deal of prior experience in making competency determinations had a great divergence. An attempt to account for these divergences would be speculative.

It is concluded that satisfactorily high interrater reliability can be attained using this instrument and its *Handbook* without extensive training. In order to insure consistently high realiability coefficients, however, the use of the *Handbook* is recommended, using a multi-observer extended series of examinations with a feedback, consensus seeking technique and with careful adherence to the interview protocol of the *Handbook* and frequent referral to its difinition section.

The validity of this instrument will rest with its utilization and acceptance in the courtroom. In a series of 15 cases before a single judge, the judge accepted the assessments of clinicians trained in the use of the instrument and used in 14 of the 15 cases. The "incorrectly" assessed patient-defendant was assessed by the clinicians as competent by audibly responded to auditory hallucinations during his court hearing.

Apart from the issue of validation of the instrument, the presiding judge accepted the instrument into evidence in each case and expert testimony was based on it. The judge made frequent reference to the items of the instrument. It would appear in this limited demonstration that the instrument was a feasible and useful means of communicating relevant, expert opinion in the competency issue for the court.

APPENDIX C

EVALUATION OF THE TRAINING PROGRAM

EVALUATION OF THE PROGRAM

Background and Procedure

Eight training sessions of one and one-half days each were held at seven State hospitals covering the major areas of the State.[1] A total of 216 trainees from various disciplines attended these eight training sessions.[2]

Prior to each training session, a list of prospective trainees was sent to the principal investigator. One-half of the randomly selected persons on this list were sent a copy of the Competency to Stand Trial Assessment Instrument (CAI) and its *Handbook* approximately one week prior to the training session. The general pattern of the training sessions involved a brief, introductory discussion of the purpose of the training and then an interview of the first patient whom the trainees rated in regard to competency. All of the patients were interviewed by the princiapl investigator using a structured interview format which generally followed the order of the items on the CAI.

The patients interviewed were persons presently at hospitals awaiting competency evaluations and subsequent court determinations. Thus, the evaluation procedure used in the present study was not merely 'a mock procedure for training but involved a real, pending legal issue.[3] The interviews were also videotaped.[4]

Following the presentation and rating of the first patient, the *Handbook* for the CAI was given to all persons who had not previously received one and there was a general discussion of the instrument and the rating of the first patient. This discussion sometimes involved a video replay of portions of the prior interview. In addition, there was a presentation of the major findings of the competency project. This was then followed by the

---

1. Two training sessions were held at Bridgewater State Hospital which handles more competency examinations than any other hospital in Massachusetts.

2. This N is based upon the number of persons who completed both the Competency to Stand Trial Assessment Instrument and the biographical information form. There were some additional persons who attended the sessions, perhaps as many as 35 to 50, from whom information was incomplete or not collected.

3. Decisions about final recommendations remained with the patients' therapists according to customary procedure.

4. Permission for these interviews was obtained from the patients and the patients' therapists in the hospital responsible for his welfare. The taping was done in view of the patient without concealment. The tapes are edited to preserve the anonymity of the patient. The facts here are not the same as in *Commonwealth* v. *Wiseman* (249 N.E. 2nd 610, 1969). This case did not prohibit the use of films for training purposes.

presentation of the second patient on the second day who was rated by the trainees. The patients were also rated by the trainers (usually three or more). After the rating of the second patient, there was a discussion of the ratings, a presentation of the Competency Screening Test, and a general discussion of competency matters.

The trainees were predominantly male and had advanced academic degrees. Forty-eight and four tenths percent were psychiatrists, 23.7 percent social workers, 12.6 percent nurses, 11.6 percent psychologists, and 3.7 percent other. Forty-three and one tenth percent had not previously participated in competency examinations, 18.1 percent had participated in 1 to 10 examinations, 18.6 percent had participated in 11 to 50 examinations, and 20.2 percent had participated in 51 to 100 or more examinations (Armor and Couch, forthcoming).[5] A few trainees, typically psychiatrists who were medical directors or superintendents of the hospitals, had participated in over 500 competency examinations. Additional information regarding trainee characteristics is given in Table 5 in the main text (page 40).

Results

Reliability: The reliability, essentially the interrater agreement among the trainees and the trainers, was evaluated primarily through the use of the intraclass R (Haggard 1968).[6] The ratings of three trainees, selected on a random basis and on a stratified random basis from each of the seven training sessions, were compared with the ratings of three trainers at each session.[7] If two or more raters observe the same patient and accurately rate this patient on specified characteristics there should be high agreement and subsequently a high intraclass R. Each patient was rated on the

---

5. Basic distribution statistics as well as subsequent analyses for skew, kurtosis, T-tests, F-tests, ETA, and linear comparisons were computed using the Data-Text 360 program, release 3, at the Harvard Computing Center. Armor, D.J., and Couch, A.S. *The Data-Text Primer: An Introduction to Computerized Social Data Analysis Using the Data-Text System.* New York: The Free Press, forthcoming.

6. The intraclass correlation coefficient is used here to assess the consistency or agreement (often, the non-independence) of scores within specific classes. This coefficient measures the relative homogeneity of scores within the classes relative to the total variation among all the scores being considered. The maximum positive coefficient is produced when there are identical scores within a class and scores differ only from class to class.

7. Three trainees were selected from each of the training sessions because the number of raters compared on a five point scale (6's were treated as no rating) markedly influenced the lower possible limits of R confirmed by earlier calculations using 20, 10 and 8 raters with this data. Haggard, *op. cit.*, pp. 18–19. The use of three trainees provides a similar base level for comparison with three trainers. Stratification was used in the study of certain variables such as prior experience. Trainees were grouped according to experience and then three trainees were randomly selected from the appropriate groups. Training data were not available from one training session (Worcester). This was an unscheduled one day training session somewhat different in format from the other sessions.

119

18 items of the CAI. There was a total of 13 patients rated; 6 before training and 7 after training.[8]

The intraclass R for the randomly selected trainees for all 13 patients was .84; the R for the trainers was .89.[9] Following training, there was a decline in rater agreement for both the trainers (.86) and trainees (.78). As noted in Table 6 (page 41 in the main text), the decline in rater agreement was somewhat greater for the trainees than for the trainers and greatest for the trainees who had not received the *Handbook*.

For the purpose of further analysis, the 13 patients were grouped by the trainers into three gross categories of degree of incompetence: (1) little or no incompetence; (2) moderate incompetence; and (3) severe incompetence. The patients were placed in these categories on the basis of trainer ratings and clinical judgment.[10] The interrater agreement of the trainers declined to .82 for moderately incompetent patients and to .79 for severely incompetent patients. Most of the disagreement seemed to center around those patients who were moderately or severely incompetent and presented widely divergent responses on the 18 items of the CAI. The trainees showed a similar decline of interrater agreement from .80 for moderately incompetent patients to .74 for severely incompetent patients.

The trainees who received a *Handbook* prior to training produced an intraclass R of .87 which was similar to that produced by trainees who had not received a *Handbook*. Following training, however, those trainees who had previously received a *Handbook* showed a considerably greater intraclass R (.85) than those who had not (.72).

To study the influence of prior experience upon interrater agreement, trainees were classified according to the number of competency examinations in which they had participated prior to the training.[11] In addition, a special sub-group of psychiatrists with 100 or more prior competency examinations (a mean of 287 examinations) was studied. These psychiatrists were generally the hospital superintendents or chief psychiatrists.

---

8. In the final training session, videotapes of four patients were played to the trainees which the trainees rated and discussed. A patient was then interviewed and rated, thus producing 7 "after" patients but only 6 "before" patients.

9. There were no significant differences between the group means of these randomly selected trainees and the means of the entire trainee group on age, education, discipline and prior examinations. Females, however, were underrepresented (29.4 percent).

10. The clinically oriented trainers were reluctant to place the patients in these categories initially solely on the basis of the patients' total scores on the 18 items of the CAI. Following the assignment of the patients to their respective categories an analysis was made of the total scores. The total scores on the CAI for patients with little or no incompetence ranged from 68–83; for patients with moderate incompetence 42–77; and for patients with severe incompetence 35–49.

11. Four categories were used: (1) no examinations; (2) 1–10 examinations; (3) 11–50 examinations; and (4) 51–100+ examinations.

When the severity of patient incompetency was controlled, prior experience showed no general pattern of influence upon the interrater reliability of the trainees. There was, however, one exception. The sub-group of highly experienced psychiatrists had an intraclass R of .61 on patients with little or no incompetence, .63 on patients with moderate incompetence, and .78 on patients with severe incompetence.

Trainer and Trainee Ratings: The ratings given to the 13 patients by the trainers and trainees on the 18 items of the CAI were examined to determine if there were consistent differences among the ratings given by various sub-groups of trainees and trainers (see Table 7, page 41 in the main text). Before training, the mean total score given to the 13 patients by the trainers was 67.7 and by the trainees was 68.6. After training, the mean total score by the trainers was 70.6 and by the trainees was 69.6 (see Table 7, page 41 in the main text). Thus, the means of the trainers and trainees were quite close. Before training, the trainees as a group tended to rate the patients as slightly more competent than the trainers and following training they tended to rate the patients slightly less competent than the trainers. Prior to the training, the trainees with the *Handbook* tended to rate patients considerably less competent than the trainees without the *Handbook*.

To conduct a more detailed study of the influence of the *Handbook*, the trainees who received it were placed in three categories according to the amount of time they spent reading it before training began: 1) less than 30 minutes; 2) 30 minutes to an hour; and 3) one hour or more (see Table 7, page 41 in the main text). Before training, there were no significant differences among these groups on the 18 items of the CAI. Following training, however, there were significant differences among the groups on 10 of the 18 items.[12] Also, the mean total scores of the three groups progressively declined with increased reading of the *Handbook*. After training, the mean of the group reading the *Handbook* one hour or more differed markedly from the mean total score of the trainers (see Table 7, page 41 in the main text).

An examination of ratings by the four major disciplines involved in the training (law was excluded because there was only one trainee who was an attorney) revealed major differences before training. Significant differences were found on 9 of the 18 CAI items.[13] T-tests and an analysis of means indicated that generally the nurses rated the patients as most competent. The next highest ratings were distributed approximately evenly between psychiatrists and social workers, and the lowest ratings of competency were

---

12. p < .05 on 3 items; p < .01 on 7 items.
13. p < .05 on 6 items; p < .01 on 3 items.

given by the psychologists.[14] The mean of the ratings by the trainers most often fell between those of the social workers and psychiatrists and seldom was as high as the nurses or as low as the psychologists.

After training, significant differences among the disciplines were found on four items.[15] The differences appeared to be less extreme and no particular discipline consistently rated the patients as most or least competent.

Prior experience, as measured by prior participation in competency examinations, was not significantly related to the receipt of a *Handbook*, but it was significantly related to age (the younger trainees had less experience),[16] to sex (the males had more experience),[17] to education (M.D.'s and Ph.D.'s had most experience),[18] and to discipline (the psychiatrists were most experienced).[19] There was no significant relationship between amount of experience and time spent reading the *Handbook*.

The trainees were grouped into four categories of experience in competency examinations: no examinations, 1-10 examination, 11-50 examinations, 51-100 examinations. Before training, there were no significant differences on any of the 18 items of the CAI (see table 7, page 41 in the main text). Following training, however, there were significant differences on 13 of the 18 items. A series of *T*-tests indicated that those persons with little or no experience most often differed significantly from the other trainees in that they tended to find the patients less competent.

Because the amount of prior experience with competency exams and the amount of time spent reading the *Handbook* seemed to influence ratings markedly after training, examination of mean total scores was made for each category of time spent and experience (see table 7, page 41 in the main text). Generally, it appears that the more time the trainees spent reading the *Handbook*, the more likely they were to rate the patients as incompetent after training. Within the three major time categories, it was generally the trainees with no experience than the trainees with very much experience who gave the lowest ratings of competency.

Discussion

The general social and legal context of the State hospitals in which the training took place was one in which there had been clear indications of inconsistent professional opinion regarding the

---

14. The psychologists rated the patients lower than any of the other three groups on 17 of the 18 items prior to training.

15. $p < .05$ on the four items.

16. $F = 7.65$, $p < .01$; linear $= 22.53$ under .001.

17. F-test $= 9.64$, $p = .001$.

18. F-test $= 7.96$, $p = .001$.

19. F-test $= 7.17$, $p = .001$.

competency of patients who had been sent for observation. Furthermore, the percentage of persons considered to be incompetent was high in these institutions. The training sought to improve the reliability of professional judgment at these hospitals and set a standard for competency recommendations consistent with common law criteria of competency and public policy.

The use of the CAI appears to have contributed considerably toward improving professional reliability. The reliability of the ratings given to the patients by the trainees (and trainers) on the CAI compares quite favorably with the reliabilities reported for similar scales.

In a survey of all major psychiatric rating scales available from 1950 to 1964, Lyerly and Abbott (1965) examined 19 commonly used scales in detail. They found that the correlation coefficients (usually Pearsonian) ranged from .31 to .92 with a mean of approximately .71 and a median of .79. The overall intraclass R of the trainees was .84 on the CAI. The trainers had an overall R of .89.

The trainers' intraclass R of .89 might be somewhat higher than usual because two of the trainers had considerable prior experience in the use of the CAI and because the trainers had the experience of rating and then mutually discussing their ratings following each of the training sessions (McGarry and Schwitzgebel 1972).[20]

The amount of agreement among the trainees and trainers was also probably greatly enhanced by the structured interviews of the 13 patients by the same trainer. On the few occasions when trainees conducted preliminary interviews, the legally relevant material necessary for accurate ratings appeared to be much more obscure or missing. High reliability on the CAI is probably dependent upon consistently structured interviews following the outline and suggested questions in the *Handbook*.

Although most trainees who received the *Handbook* read it for 30 minutes or more, it alone did not seem to influence interrater reliability. Trainees with and without the *Handbook* obtained similar R's (.87) before training. After training, however, which required close attention to the rating system, those persons with the *Handbook* had considerably better interrater agreement (R of .85) than those without the *Handbook* (R of .72).

A more detailed examination of several specific sub-groups of trainees suggests that the training had a differential impact on the trainees. Generally, the training does not appear to have increased agreement between the trainees and the trainers. In fact, the overall scores are more divergent following training than before training.

It also appears that two of the groups which tended to give the lowest ratings of competency were those with very little or no experience in competency examinations and those with very much

---

20. This use of feedback of scores and consensus seeking produced an R of .92 over a series of 18 patients for 3 trainers in a previous study.

experience (see Table 7, page 41 in the main text). After training, these two groups tended to give ratings which were more divergent from the trainers' ratings than before training.

Why the training apparently produced some results opposite of those intended is a matter of speculation. Those trainees with no prior experience may have been sensitized by the training to look for incompetency — perhaps as a means of demonstrating expertise. Those trainees with very much experience (generally psychiatrists) who were interested enough in the problem of competency to spend one hour or more reading the *Handbook* may have been a group with a high base rate of expectation of incompetency. In situations of clinical ambiguity (the patients presented after training tended to have more complex patterns of response), they may have used a decision strategy reflecting this high base rate of expectancy. Of course, it is also possible that other biases may have influenced the outcomes of the least experienced trainees. If such a bias was operative, the training did not effectively mitigate it.

Conclusions

The use of the CAI with interviews structured around the 18 items of the scale produced satisfactorily high interrater reliability without extensive training. Patients who were not incompetent or were mildly incompetent were more reliably rated than those extremely incompetent.

The reading of the *Handbook* alone did not influence reliability either positively or negatively. When, however, the reading of the *Handbook* was combined with the experience of rating patients during training, those trainees who had read the *Handbook* showed reliability considerably superior to those trainees who had not read it.

Training was not, however, completely successful. Generally, the overall scores of the trainees were more divergent from the scores of the trainers following training than before training. Also, the training may have had a differential impact upon specific subgroups of trainees. For example, trainees with little or no prior experience in competency examinations who studied the *Handbook* over 30 minutes gave patients markedly lower ratings of competency than did the trainers following training, but not before training. The training may have potentiated a sensitivity to incompetency or a self-selection bias may have been operating in which persons most likely to find incompetency in the patients presented after training also chose to spend the greatest amount of time studying the *Handbook*. The limited training failed to produce the desired outcome.

The reliability and external validity of the CAI as found in this preliminary research would seem to warrant further study and clinical investigation. The *Handbook* appears to be a useful adjunct. The nature of training which should accompany the use of the CAI to increase its reliability is not clear but might involve the feedback of ratings and consensus seeking by the trainees over an extended series of patients. This method of establishing reliability had been successful among project staff members in their work with the CAI. The brief training sessions of the type described above do not appear to be adequate.

INDEX

influence of project in, 47
pretrial competency procedures in, 3
projects results being implemented in,
    projects results being implemented in,
    3, 16-17
survey of commitments by courts of,
    55-56
Massachusetts Defenders Committee (Public
    Defenders), 19, 48, 54, 58
Massachusetts District Courts, 57-59
Massachusetts District Misdemeanor Courts,
    57
Massachusetts General Laws
    Chapter III of, Section 24A, 8
    Chapter 123 of
        Section 17, 56
        Sections 100 and 105, 14
        Section 100A, 62
Massachusetts legislature, 48
Massachusetts State Hospitals
    intercurrent statistical changes at,
        prior to enactment of Mental Health
        Reform Act, 49-54
    number of pretrial examinations in (1963;
        1972), v
    See also Bridgewater State Hospital
"Massachusetts Statutory and Case Law on
    Competency to Stand Trial" (Rosenberg),
    39
Massachusetts Superior Courts, 59
Massachusetts Supreme Judicial Court, rulings
    of
    Commonwealth v. *Druken*, 48n, 53-57
    Nason v. *Superintendent of Bridgewater State
        Hospital*, 58
    Petition of Rohrer, 14, 36, 37, 48n, 55,
        59-61
Matthews, A. R., 2, 46
Medical criteria used to determine
    incompetency, 1
Mental Disability and the Criminal Law
    (Matthews), 46
Mental Health, Department of (Mass.), 53-55,
    61
Mental health professionals, training of,
    16-17, 19
    CAI used in, 17, 39, 42, 118, 120, 121, 123,
        124
Mental Health Program Reports (NIMH), 59
Mental Health Reform Act (1970), iv,
    6-7, 17, 18, 48-54, 60, 67
    intercurrent statistical changes in
        Massachusetts State Hospitals
        prior to enactment of, 49-54
Mental institutions, communication between
    courts and, 66-67; *see also specific
    institutions; for example:* Bridgewater
    State Hospital
Mental retardation
    competence and, 14, 100
    paucity of law dealing with, 6
Metropolitan State Hospital (Calif.), 2-3
Metropolitan State Hospital (Mass.), 17, 55
Minnesota Multiphasic Personality Inventory
    (MMPI), 13, 22, 32, 94
Morris, N., iii, 9
Motivation, self-defeating v. self-serving
    clinical examples of, 113-14
    defined, 103
Multiple-observer consensus-seeking
    technique, 19

Nash (justice), 57
Nason, 58
Nason v. *Superintendent of Bridgewater
    State* (1968), 58
National Institute of Mental Health (NIMH),
    9, 10, 14, 59
Nationwide commitments (1970), 2n
New York State, effects of *Baxtrom* v.
    Herold in, 60
NIMH (National Institute of Mental Health),
    9, 10, 14, 59
Northampton State Hospital (Mass.), 17

Observational commitments
    base rates of valid, 65
    basis for, 57
    following screening examinations, 65-66
    in 1970, 2n
Oppergard, C. R., 1

Papers published following project, 38-39
Paranoid schizophrenia, 33
Pate v. *Robinson* (1966), 2n, 58n
Pension product-moment correlations
    between CST and other tests, 94-95
Penalties, appreciation of range and nature
    of
    clinical examples of, 109-10
    defined, 102
Pertinent facts, capacity to disclose to
    attorneys, 102
    clinical examples of, 111-12
    defined, 102
Petition of Harman, 59n
Petition of Rohrer (1967), 14
    36, 37, 48n, 55, 59-61
Posttrial attorney protocols, 12, 13, 54
Posttrial defendant protocols, 12, 13
Posttrial interview protocols, 12
Posttrial observation protocols, 13
Predictive accuracy of CST, 34-35, 93-94
Pretrial commitments, *see* Commitments
Pretrial screenings, 13-14
    automatic, 62-63
    in D.C., 46
    importance of, 18
    1972, ix
    procedure to follow for, 65
    purpose of, 4
    See also Competency Screening Test
Preventive detention
    bail laws and, 53
    risks of, 18
"Problems of public consultation in
    medico-legal matters" (McGarry,
    Curran and Kenefick), 38
Project
    conclusions and products of, 4-7
    5-year plan for, 10-16
    problems studied in, 1-3
    significance and scope of, 62-63
    specific objectives of, 3
Project population, 23, 89-90
Projective tests, 11
Prosecuting attorneys, appraising role of
    clinical examples of, 107
    defined, 102
Prosecution witnesses, capacity to
    challenge
    clinical examples of, 112
    defined, 102-3

130

Protection against self-incrimination, 10
Protocols
  attorneys posttrial, 12, 13, 54
  courtroom observation
    purpose of, 12
    role of psychiatrists and attorneys
      in, 13
  posttrial defendant, 12, 13
  posttrial interview, 13
  posttrial observation, 12
Psychiatric decompensation, 45
"Psychiatric examination of alleged
    offenders" (Bendt, Balcanoff and
    Tragellis), 38
"Psychiatrist in a Superior Court
    Setting, The" (Balcanoff), 38
Psychiatrists
  check lists developed by, 45
  effective function of, 4
  as experts on competency, 63-65
  protectionist bias of, 18
  role of, in second year of project, 12,
    13
Psychiatry, improving communication between
    law and, CAI and, 23-24
Psychologists, role of, in second year of
    project, 12-13
Psychomotor test, CST, as, 32-33
Psychoses
  as basis for incompetency, 12, 100
  scoring of MMPI and, 32
Public Defenders (Massachusetts Defenders
    Committee), 19, 48, 54, 58
Public Health Commissioner of Massachusetts,
    authority of, 8-9
Punishment, sense of guilt and, 46

Quantifiable clinical criteria, developing,
    as purpose of study, 3

Ratings of trainees, 121
Reforms, necessary and recommended, 65-67
Rehabilitation, providing opportunities for,
    18
Relating to attorneys, quality of
  clinical examples of, 105
  defined, 101
Richardson, Elliott, 60
Robey, A., 36, 45
Rohrer, 36
"Role of the psychiatrist in pretrial
    examinations, The" (Balcanoff and
    McGarry), 38
Rorschach Test, 13, 22, 94-95
Rosenberg, A. H., 38, 39, 59, 60
Rotated factor loadings of CST, 28-30,
    90
Rotter, J. B., 27
Roxbury District Court (Mass.), 54
Rugg (justice), 63
Rule 74 (Massachusetts District Court),
    57-58

Scheidemandel, P.L., iii, 2
Schiele, B. C., 32
Schizophrenia
  paranoid, 33
  percentage of, in project population,
    89, 91
Schwitzgebel, R. K., 9, 39

Scoring
  on CAI, 19, 24-25, 33-34, 101
  on CST, 27-28, 33-34
  on CRAT, 27
  on Graham Kendall, 32-33
Screenings, see Pretrial screenings
Segal, J., 59
Self-defeating v. self-serving motivation
    (legal sense)
  clinical examples of, 113-14
  defined, 103
Self-incrimination, protection against,
    10
Sense of guilt, punishment and, 46
Sentence completion method, value of, 27
Settle, R. D., 1
Shah, S. A., v
Sixth Amendment (1791), 56
Social Responsibility Test, 11, 13, 22
Special Commission on Mental Health
    (Massachusetts Legislature), 48, 59
Speedy trials
  effects of Jackson v. Indiana decision on,
    56
  positive effects of, 18
Spiegel (justice), 57
Statute of limitations, applied at time
    of finding incompetency, 66
"Statutory and Case Law Survey on Competency
    to Stand Trial" (Bender), 39
Stotsky-Weinberg instrument, 11
Suffork Superior Criminal Court
    (Mass.), 10, 25, 115
Supreme Court, rulings of, 48, 56-57

Taunton State Hospital (Mass.), 17
Tauro (chief justice), 14, 37
Thematic Apperception Test (TAT), 11, 26
Thomas, T. E., 1
"Titicut Follies revisited: A long-range
    plan for the mentally disordered
    offender in Massachussetts" (McGarry),
    38
Tragellis, G. S., 38
Trainees, ratings of, 121-22
Trainers, ratings of, 121-22
Training, 16-19, 29, 31
  evaluating, 39-42, 118-25
Trials, see Speedy trials

Unmanageable behavior
  clinical examples of, 104-5
  defined, 101

Van Buskirk, C., 27

Wechsler Adult Intelligence Scale (WAIS),
    13, 22, 32, 94
Weinberg (doctor), 11
Wiley, E. D., 61
Willerman, B., 27
Witnesses
  appraising role of
    clinical examples of, 107
    defined, 102
  capacity to challenge prosecution
    clinical examples of, 112
    defined, 102-3
Wittenberg, Mrs. Ralph, 59

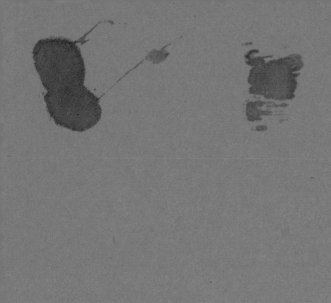

rk 10003